About the

Born in Northumberland, Jo Goodwin-Worton lives in Staffordshire with her Husband Gareth who she married in 2022. Jo is a proud mother to two grown up sons, a step-daughter and step-son.

In 2018, Jo's life changed forever when her late husband Jay was diagnosed with Stage Four Gastro-Oesophageal cancer. After a brave and valiant battle with the disease, Jay sadly died thirteen months later.

It was after her bereavement that Jo took a brave leap of faith in her life. She enrolled on a BA (Hons) Psychological Studies Degree at University. She gained an Advanced Diploma in Thanatology and Bereavement Counselling, as well as other relevant academia, in order to change her career and use her experience to help other people who are grieving due to a loss or bereavement.

Jo is now a qualified Grief Specialist; she runs her own business 'Seeds in Time', providing grief support and grief training.

Jo's debut book 'Caring for Cancer the Real Journey' was released in May 2022 with readers commending its raw honesty and inspirational outlook.

Back to Normal?

Jo Goodwin-Worton

This edition first published in paperback by
Michael Terence Publishing in 2023
www.mtp.agency

ISBN 9781800945500

Michael Terence
Publishing

Acknowledgements

Contributors: Your contribution is integral to making this book so heartfelt and so real. I am honoured to include each story, your experiences at times brought me to tears, at the same time I feel incredibly privileged that you trusted me to tell your story. I feel so blessed to have been given an insight into your lives, I truly believe it has made me a better person, both personally and professionally.

Lewis and Oliver: I always knew you would be extraordinary young men and you have proved that to me time and time again. Your stoicism and passion for life is truly heart-warming and makes me so proud. I will always believe that you are both my greatest achievement in life. I love you both so much.

Gareth: You have always believed in me and your support is more than I could have ever wished for. You have taught me to never let go of who I am and to never lose sight of that impossible dream, even when I doubt myself. You have always embraced my past, allowing me to nurture my emotional scars rather than covering them up. You love my fiery independence, but at the same time you are the person I rely on when I feel like the 'pedestal is too high and I feel like I'm falling'. I am so proud to be your wife and your best friend, and I cannot wait to see where life takes us both figuratively and geographically!

Sarah: You have been there for me throughout the last twenty (plus) years and never once have you ever doubted me or let me fall when I have been at my lowest. Equally we have shared the most amazing fun times and laughed so much, mostly over a couple of bottles of wine! Never doubt how amazing you are Sarah; you are the most wonderful person and anyone who meets you is immensely lucky, never be afraid to take a leap of faith, as you just never know where life will take you.

Paul: You are one of my best friends, my essay/book editor and the person who always tells me to keep achieving my dreams! When my grammar is terrible or I lose my way, you are always there for me with some encouraging advice and motivation to inspire me to keep going. Your support and friendship means so much to me.

Contents

Introduction

What is loss and grief? Truth is, it is different for everyone as we all experience life in our own unique way; however, I do like a good metaphor and this one seemed to capture the feelings perfectly.

"The experience of loss and grief are like vast emotional waves which just keep coming towards you, they often seem relentless and at times you wonder how on earth you will survive.

Like the ocean sometimes the 'grief' waves are smaller and more manageable, but sometimes they represent an emotional tsunami which seems impossible to even imagine, never mind overcome.

Eventually, one day you notice the ferocity of the storm has lessened, and the sea is calmer, however in a moment those waves return and reawaken those painful emotions and feelings.

After a bereavement and in time, you start to notice that as you experience those 'waves', they seem less ferocious and overwhelming. Over time you build up a level of stoicism and resilience and although they are still difficult, you weather each storm with a little bit more confidence.

In the early days of a bereavement especially, life moves in slow motion, you can see the people around you and you can hear the words they are speaking but in reality, you often have no comprehension of what to do, how to react and how to feel. There is a sense of numbness, the life you knew feels as if it has just irrefutably changed and now all you can do is breathe, but even that seems impossible as you take each breath in. Comprehending the gravity of this new world you are now living in is difficult and knowing what to do, what to say is sometimes incomprehensible. You know you should say and do something but what can you say, and what can you do? Your brain is like a dense fog clouding the ability to talk coherently, and has no idea on how to begin to string a sentence together.

Physically, there are times when you try to move your body but the pain is overwhelming, yet you look down and you are not hurt or injured, there are no reasons for that pain to be there, but the pain is real and the pain is agonising.

People around you are asking you questions and expecting you to have the answer straight away nonetheless those words suddenly seem unimportant and all you crave is silence. The pain can be like a fire in your veins and your stomach feels like it's going to burst with the reality of what is happening. You want to cry but you know if you do you won't stop and you know if you do that people will say those common words which everyone seems to say, "are you okay". Truth is you are definitely, NOT okay! The world needs to stop turning so that you can focus on simply breathing and coming to terms with the enormity of this life changing event, maybe if it did stop, just for a few moments you could regain a sense of composure, but, sadly as we all know, that is something out of our control.

In essence, dealing with loss and grief can be like learning to recognise that sometimes the 'waves' of life don't stop, but what I have discovered after my own grief is that over time, we somehow find that inner strength and when those 'waves' hit us although we feel every emotion of the loss, we stand as strong as we can. Finding that strength is about regaining a level of control over our loss and grief, which isn't easy, but is possible. Like anything it doesn't happen overnight, it's something which happens over time and the journey certainly isn't a straight road, just as you move forward you may be drawn backwards, but essentially you are always moving towards the future.

A loss or bereavement is all of the above and so much more, however every single experience is unique, my journey is different to yours and your journey is different to another person's. We simply cannot precisely define specifically how a person reacts to a bereavement or loss and how they grieve. What is universal however, is that there are no right or wrong answers, we all find our way through, and we all have our own coping strategies and approaches.

If you have been through a loss or bereavement does this all sound familiar? We are all diverse and we all experience life very differently, but collectively we all have a voice and if we use that voice to help people understand what the 'real journey' is like I believe it becomes just that little bit less scary.

So, how is it possible to even contemplate moving on? The answer lies in each of us individually but sharing our stories and our experiences helps us to understand that we are not alone and that it is okay to not be okay, and that the common response of 'you'll get back to normal soon' can be thrown out the window so that we can make our own meaningful steps forward into a different world.

Through an inspiring and emotional journey of some very different real-life stories, I have reflected on how loss and/or bereavement is a very personal journey to each person with everyone experiencing it in their own different way, this is reflected in each and every story through-out this book.

I chose to include stories of loss as well as bereavement in the book as I believe it is important to capture the importance and significance of how a loss can be just as distressing as a bereavement. It is widely assumed that when we talk about 'a loss' that it is to do with a death, however a loss can also be life-changing too.

Reader Information

All names and locations have been changed throughout the book to protect true identities; however, the stories are factual and are real lived experiences.

In order to keep the book as authentic as possible please be aware that the stories at times may be distressing or contain descriptive details of conditions and/or experiences. If these stories do trigger memories for you, or you find you need extra support, please do seek further advice and support.

There are many different options of support you can source in relation to coping with grief and bereavement. If you feel you need support with your loss or grief, grief support counselling can offer a safe and non-judgement space for you to talk about your experiences. An experienced and qualified bereavement counsellor will offer the time and space to actively listen and offer bespoke professional support.

Alongside the counselling and training services I offer through 'Seeds in Time,' there are also some truly exceptional charities who also offer professional and supportive advice. All are helpful, and offer both emotional and practical support at a very difficult time. I would also strongly recommend accessing services through your GP or local support networks who can offer professional and suitable therapeutic support, if required.

For information on the services offered by Seeds in Time whether that be individual counselling, group support or grief training please visit: www.seedsintime.co.uk

I

Life, Loss, Bereavement and the Future

Throughout our lives we go through many trials and tribulations, most thankfully are pleasant and fulfilling, we wake up each morning not knowing what the day will bring and we go to sleep each night thinking of the day that was. We have an element of control in our lives but there are some things that are simply beyond our remit.

The occurrence of a loss can be uncontrollable and unavoidable, it could be something relatively simple or it could be something which is life-changing. Depending on the loss in question, it can potentially affect an individual's physical health, emotional health and/or their psychological health on varying levels of intensity.

When a person dies it is another of those times where life just seems so very unfair, especially when the person who dies is someone we love or care about.

Death is a word that is often avoided, it's very mention brings about an undesirable feeling of unrest and uneasiness and yet it is something which will happen to every living human being on the planet, we are born and at some point, we will die, it is probably the only two certainties in life which are guaranteed. Whilst most people live to an impressive old age and die of natural causes there are of course those sad times when a death is unexpected or beyond our control, in both children and adults.

So, why are we so scared of death and dying if it is inevitable? Unfortunately, there is not a singular universal answer to that question, and it is fraught with different meanings which encompass a person's personal, cultural, spiritual, and religious beliefs. What we do know is that when someone dies it is the living who deal with the emotional consequences and that is where bereavement and grief find their place in our lives.

Most people do tend to gravitate away from their feelings about death as they are perceived as inherently negative and something that we don't need to think about yet, after all why would we think about death when we are so busy trying to actually live life in the present!

Death however is not perceived by all as negative, there are religious and cultural beliefs across the world that see death as a new beginning of life, and that when a person dies their spirit is re-born and lives on eternally. The human physical body is seen as a vessel for which our physica form inhabits, but the spirit is what makes us who we are and guides us into the next living world after the human body is no longer able to sustain life. This spiritual belief can be of incredible comfort to many and offers a sense of hope in the quest for eternal life and finding a meaningful living ex stence.

Death as a subject of discussion can be a very thought-provoking conversation and forms a unique and important part of our life, full of many viewpoints and opinions. I have often started a conversation with people about mortality and I am often struck by the diversity of the answers I receive. Throughout my childhood I remember seeing movies and tv programmes depicting fictional stories of finding the answers to immortality, I was always fascinated about how eternal life was seen as the ultimate goal by some people.

Out of personal interest I asked twenty people one question and recorded their answers anonymously. The question was "If you had the option would you like to live forever? Out of the twenty people every single person said 'No', they would not want to live forever. This study was a very small cohort and cannot be used as a definitive hypothesis, however it was interesting to hear that not one person said yes, and yet, we continue to avoid talking about death still, even though my question shows that most people do not actually desire immortality and therefore accept the fact that one day they will die.

I was sent a message afterwards by one of the contributors to that question which really made me think as their message was incredibly poignant, it said "living forever would be amazing, but it means that I would need to experience the death of every single person I love, every family member, friend, colleague and acquaintance, how many times can a heart be broken until the heart itself becomes completely broken. I would rather live my life and experience love within my natural lifetime than an eternal life of possible heartache."

Later, I asked about what images are associated with the word 'Death', I asked my Husband what images he would think of when asked to describe 'death', he said "sadness, darkness, black, empty, nothing". Another friend I asked said "a coffin, people crying, loss and sadness". I then asked another friend whose response surprised me, I asked the same question and they said "sadness but also a celebration of that person's life, death is a way of reminding us to appreciate those around us and to really be grateful for just living." Their response although not typical was a reminder of how we are all different in our viewpoints and our thoughts on death and dying. There is no 'normal' answer to this question, it will change from person to person, nevertheless I was moved by her uplifting and positive interpretation.

Death is a fact of life, and most people accept that fact, however I think the important point here is to appreciate that although it may be inevitable it is much more important to actually focus on living and enjoying life in the very best way we can. In the future we will all have a date we were born and a date we died, but have we ever considered the story in between those dates? The life we lead between our birth and death can be very different but can also be exciting filled with thousands of different stories and adventures.

Life though, as we all know, is rather like a rollercoaster, it has many ups and downs. It sometimes goes at a slow pace and is uneventful, at other times it is faster and more hectic; that is the nature of life as we know it. Life is unique to each and every one of us and how we experience, and feel about our lives is something which is hard to accurately put into words. The uniqueness and sheer individuality of every person means that it is hard to assume how someone feels about a loss or bereavement.

Whilst it is true that we all share personality traits which may be similar after a bereavement or loss, the terms 'normal response' and 'normal reactions' I feel, are certainly open to individual interpretation.

My own experience of bereavement and grief has certainly been an emotional journey of self-discovery and personal insight. I had no idea what was 'expected' and how you should act after someone you love dies. The initial thoughts about grief are that people are crying and that you might be angry or in denial about the death, yet that's not always the case, I certainly had my own way of dealing with grief. What I am sure about is that there is no right or wrong way to grieve.

After Jay passed away in 2019, his death started a journey for me that I could never have even contemplated. It was life changing for so many different reasons from both a negative and positive perspective. Is that normal? Then again, what is normal? Are my feelings and emotions the same as the 'standard' emotions labelled as a normal person grieving? When you experience a loss or bereavement you can have many conflicting thoughts, but what I can definitively say is that not one of those feelings or emotions are wrong, they are our bespoke and individual response to grief.

When Jay was initially diagnosed, I remember being instantly confronted with the thought of death and dying. Those first thought processes are instantly negative and despite the positive attitude you aspire to portray it can be impossible to contain the emotion, and the overriding feelings of sadness. It can be incredibly scary at first and finding the strength to talk and open up about grief can feel overwhelming, yet it can also be the one thing that supports you on your journey and allows you to find a meaningful way forward into a different 'new-normal' future.

For me personally, it was the first time in my life where I had to really confront the possibility of losing someone I loved. I had previously experienced bereavement with the loss of Grandparents, various pets, and distant family members but this loss felt more intense and more emotionally traumatic. It is incredibly hard to truly put into words how you feel and to describe the emotions you feel when confronted with the thought of a loved one's mortality, especially in those earlier days when the news is so numbing.

In those early days you can feel physically nauseous and light-headed, your body feels incredibly heavy, like your legs can't carry the weight of you. You naturally take each breath, yet you also feel as if you cannot catch your breath, it's like someone has punched you in the stomach and the throat; it feel's painful and incapacitating. As you try to overcome those feelings it can often lead to hyper-ventilating, or panic attacks. Whilst these symptoms are not life-threatening, they are distressing. The good news, is that they do subside and you do learn to breathe through the bad times.

There are times in the initial hours, days and weeks after a loss or bereavement that you feel that you want to cry, but the tears are just not there, your eyes can feel heavy and sore and closing them can weirdly seem wrong. You want to believe that it's just an awful nightmare, and you will wake up and it would all go away.

After receiving bad news, your head tries to think logically and knows it needs to ask questions to gain the facts which will enable you to process the information and to prepare you for what comes next, however what actually happens is that your brain goes blank as it's all too much to process in that moment of time.

What is deemed as 'normal' at this moment in time, is definitely open to interpretation and there is simply no definitive answer. Anyone who has experienced a loss or bereavement I'm sure will agree that trying to accurately describe it, is incredibly difficult.

Everyone experiences loss in a different way but the death of a loved one can be one of great sadness and loneliness. Your world initially stops and when it starts turning again, it's different than it was before. Your life continues but you don't know how to keep going, you hear the comforting words people are saying to you and see the love they are showing you, however you can't comprehend anything, nothing at all makes sense and merely seeing past the end of the day seems impossible at first.

So, how is it possible to even contemplate moving on from the thought of losing someone we love and/or dealing with the loss, bereavement and associated grief? The answer lies in each of us individually but sharing our stories and our experiences helps us to understand that we are not alone and that it is okay to not be okay and that the common response of 'you'll get back to normal soon' is exceedingly debateable.

To be able to provide a wide-ranging account of loss, grief, and bereavement, I spoke with a diverse group of people and asked them if they would mind talking to me about their experience and to talk in their own uncensored words about their journey through loss, bereavement, or grief. Their stories at times brought me to tears and I was so grateful for their honesty and how strong they were in talking so openly about their feelings and emotions.

To protect those who contributed, I have changed their identify including all names and any information which could identify them, however their words are their own and offer a raw and personal insight into their experience.

I was astounded by the stoicism and resilience each person disclosed and how ultimately, they used their experience to shape their own unique future and whilst these stories are sometimes sad, they show a remarkable level of hope which in all the stories is both inspirational and truly heartening.

2

True Love

My first lady is truly extraordinary with her story being so moving that just writing it left me in tears on many occasions. It was an absolute honour to talk to her and to have the pleasure of hearing her story which she told so eloquently.

Diana is an 81-year-old woman, her husband Bobby died two years ago of a brain haemorrhage one evening while they were at home. They had just celebrated their 60th wedding anniversary in the month previous and were looking forward to the birth of their first Great-Grandchild the following month. Diana agreed to talk to me about her experience of sudden bereavement and how she has coped with the loss of her Husband. The story is written in Diana's own words, as she spoke so powerfully about Bobby that it really gives a deeper appreciation for the love they shared.

Diana's Story

"I met Bobby at a Saturday night dance, I remember seeing him across the hall, he was very handsome, and I knew straight away he was the one for me. We courted for a while but soon after he proposed, and we married the year after. We were blessed with three children over the following years, two girls and a boy.

We had a very good life. I worked as a seamstress whilst looking after our children and Bobby worked as an

Electrician. We never had a lot of money but we had a comfortable life and Bobby always made sure we never went without; he was a proud man and always worked hard to give the children a good upbringing. He was an old-romantic at heart and always brought me a bunch of flowers on a Friday night, although I think that's because I used to never moan about him going to the local pub first for a couple of pints with his work friends.

We had so many lovely holidays, mostly in the UK as we couldn't really afford to go abroad but we loved travelling around finding new places to visit. We made so many lovely memories with the children. When the children were grown up, they started their own families and we were delighted when our grandchildren arrived, we were ',over the moon'.

We were generally blessed with good health most of our lives, apart from the normal age-related aches and pains but 'that week', Bobby had complained about a nagging headache which was bothering him but we thought nothing of it, and he just took some Aspirin. On the Tuesday night I remember Bobby got up from his chair but then immediately collapsed and fell to the floor. It all happened in slow motion, it was like time was standing still and at first, I froze as I looked at him lying on the floor motionless. It was 8.22pm as I looked at the clock, that time is forever in my thoughts now. I called the ambulance and they tried to talk me through CPR as he lay on the floor but it was really hard as I could hardly get onto the floor, and when I did, I was scared to hurt him when they were telling me what to do. I remember listening to the lady on the end of the phone, but I knew he was gone. I tried everything but, in the end, I just hung up the phone. I just sat with him until the paramedics arrived in complete silence. I rubbed his hand and straightened his hair, he was still so handsome, like the day I met him, just with a few more wrinkles, but to me he was perfect. I remember not crying though, I didn't know what to do, it was like it wasn't real, like a dream.

I remember the two paramedics coming in and there being lots of things happening but it's all such a blur, I remember them having lots of machines and things but then after a few minutes, they stopped and sat down next to me and just said 'we are so sorry, he's gone'. I didn't want to believe them. He was 'my Bobby', he was the only man I had ever loved, he was 'my Bobby'. I gave the paramedic my address book and they rang my eldest daughter for me.

My daughter took care of things for me after she arrived, I didn't know what to do but I do remember the funeral directors arriving to take Bobby away.

It felt strange, like I would wake up and my Bobby would be sitting next to me, like he was coming in from work or if he had popped to the kitchen. My son arrived and I remember him making me a cup of tea and then holding my hand. He was crying but I felt confused and I didn't know what to do. We sat there and although they were all talking, I had no idea what they were speaking about as my mind was all funny. I stared at the chair where he had been sitting and then again at the carpet where he had fell. I didn't understand how in the space of one evening my life had changed and it was now forever different. The house felt quiet, it felt empty.

I don't know what time it was but I remember feeling tired, my daughter and son had left to get back to their children and I was then alone. I sat in the dark with just the lamp on for light, I kept thinking 'in a minute Bobby would walk through the door' as if he had just been to the kitchen to put the kettle on, he would then sit down and watch the TV. We would enjoy a cup of tea and we would talk and laugh at whatever was on the television.

He didn't come through the door though and in that moment, I started crying. I cried so hard I couldn't breathe, my chest hurt, my eyes hurt, everything hurt. I must have fallen asleep on the chair as I woke up and it was early morning. I remember, I was holding his house jacket when I woke, I must have fallen asleep with it. It smelt like him still, Old Spice, oh how I hated it, but I remember suddenly thinking it smelt lovely.

I think about my Bobby every single day, I sometimes think I feel him close to me, like he's looking after me but I'm not sure. I talk to his photo every day and I tell him off for leaving me, I tell him off for not saying goodbye too. Whenever he went out or when we went to bed, he always used to say, 'I love You'. I just wanted to tell him I love him even if it was one last time.

I understand he's not here, but I don't understand why he didn't get the chance to say goodbye.

I miss him every day, when I wake up, he's the first person I think about, I turn over in bed and he's not there. The children come to see me and they do occasionally talk about him, but they have their own families now, I don't want to bother them with me being silly, I don't want to be a burden to them.

Life isn't the same though, it's not like it was before, I feel very lonely these days, and everything reminds me of him, even down to watching the news or picking up the morning newspaper. Life before he died was simple, it was good, but I know deep down we all have our time, and this was Bobby's.

When I die, I hope we will be together again, I know he will be waiting for me as I know he didn't want to leave me, he had no choice but I still don't understand, I wish I had left before him so I didn't have to live without him, but I think that's selfish too as I wouldn't want him to be sad either.

I have a good life don't get me wrong, I love my family, but I miss Bobby so much, I just want to be with him. The other day my friend came to visit and we were laughing at an old memory about the time we went on holiday to Wales and Bobby fell over in the sea trying to impress the children. It was lovely to smile, but I feel sometimes guilty for being happy some days, but he wouldn't want me to be sad all the time, in fact he would probably tell me off if he were here. The good days are good but the sad days, not so great.

I am looking forward to seeing my Great-Grandchild grow up, my family are the reason I smile these days, I love them dearly, I tell them about their Grandad, and I tell them of all our stories, I'm not sure if they understand as they are quite young still, but I love talking about Bobby and keeping his memory alive. Bobby will always be with me in my heart, until we meet again."

Diana's story is one which may resonate with many of our elderly communities. After over sixty years together it was almost as if Diana and Bobby had merged to become one person instead of two, they lived their life through each other and never really contemplated ever being apart.

What is poignant about Diana's story is that she was very aware of her grief and was not in denial about the fact that Bobby had died, but she was still grieving his loss every single day. The manner of Bobby's death was one of great upset to Diana too as she never had the chance to say goodbye, so she had no way of preparing herself emotionally for the loss of the love of her life.

Through speaking with Diana, it transpired that she had never really spoke to anyone about her feelings or thoughts after Bobby's death. Diana did not want to burden anyone with her troubles and felt that she would eventually 'get over' it. For Diana to share her story with me I was overwhelmed by her bravery, with her courage to talk so openly being both inspiring and for Diana quite cathartic.

After that initial conversation I have spent many hours with Diana just listening to her talk and to this day I still visit her and, she still shares her stories with me. When Diana tells me her many stories she smiles as she says Bobby's name and takes great pride in remembering him and their precious time together. Does she still have her bad days? Absolutely. Does she still experience sadness on special occasions and memorable dates? Unquestionably. The unconditional love for Bobby will never leave Diana, however she finds comfort in believing that one day they will be reunited, in the meantime, she is grateful for the love of her family and friends.

Diana's story has undoubtedly reminded me of my grief. Diana was with Bobby for many years, and she has taught me so much throughout our conversations. What we both learnt was that talking makes grief that little bit easier to deal with. Talking is part of the grieving journey and is a powerful aid to finding a way forward. She has been and will always be such an inspiration to me, she has taught me so much and I am eternally grateful for meeting her and hearing her story.

I believe grief is multidimensional, it doesn't come in a 'one size fits all' model, instead, everyone experiences it in their own unique way, with there being no real right or wrong way to grieve. However, there is one important and shared factor to consider when it comes to grief and that is that it does not dissipate or even get smaller over time, it stays the same. Instead, it is a person's life which grows around the grief and that is essentially how we learn to carry on and find a meaningful future.

In Diana's case, she will always mourn the death of Bobby, every single day she remembers the life they had, but she has found her own way of living alongside her bereavement to remember their wonderful time together. Her life now although different has a new direction and a sense of 'new-normal' which she embraces, alongside her new passion; her adopted dog, Sandy, who has brought both companionship and happiness into her life.

3

Loss

A definition of loss is defined in the English Dictionary as "The fact of no longer having something or having less of it than before". *(Collins English Dictionary, 2022).*

The meaning of 'a loss' is quite subjective; it can be explained in so many varied ways and have several different interpretations in relation to exactly what it means. Whilst the majority of people may associate loss predominately with a bereavement, essentially it means *(as the dictionary describes)* 'losing something which is important or significant', so that could be a job, a house, money, or friendship, to name just a few. In fact, loss is quite an idiosyncratic term given that it is unique to every person; how we feel and interpret the consequences of a loss is not strictly measurable. Instead it is based on individual perception, feelings, and emotions based on the nature and proximity of the loss.

Thinking about loss specifically and looking back on my own personal life, I have had many losses throughout the years, more than I initially realised until I sat down and really thought about it. Some were small losses which I recovered from quite quickly, other losses were more significant and therefore stood out more as an emotional event within my life.

It is only when we stop and recollect our life in more detail that we can start to appreciate what we have all been through and the roller-coaster of emotions we experience throughout our lives.

Task → This task is an insightful and reflective exercise to do but one which can be incredibly rewarding. On a piece of paper or digitally, compile a timeline from the moment you were born until the present day. It resembles a long line which has dates on the top of the line and the corresponding losses on the bottom of the line. You can start from birth and end with the current date, completing the timeline as best as you can remember.

The number of entries on the timeline is personal to you so there are no right or wrong answers to this task. On that timeline mark down all the losses you have encountered throughout your life, these could be any of the following below, however this list is not exhaustive as loss is a very personal feeling so just write down what you feel you have 'lost'.

- Death of someone you loved/or someone you knew
- Loss of a job
- Loss of a house/home/place of interest
- Loss of faith
- Loss of wellbeing/health (physical or mental health)

<u>*Example*</u>

25.3.99	31.8.15	17.1.20	29.3.21	14.12.21
Father Died	Lost Job	Dog Died	Medical Diagnosis	Made Redundant

Again, this list is only a reflection of what you could include as everyone's experience of loss is different and there is no right or wrong way to complete this task. When you have completed your timeline, sit and reflect on your life and how many losses you have experienced. Are you surprised by how many or how little there are? How did they affect you at the time? Do they still affect you now?

It is quite a powerful exercise to do, and it may evoke some strong feelings and emotions, however the overall aim of this exercise is to show that throughout our lives we all experience some level of loss which doesn't have to always be associated with a bereavement. Life is certainly not linear; it is full of both inevitability and ambiguity. What is also important to recognise is that despite those losses in your life, you did get through them, and you did find a way through those difficult feelings to be where you are today. At the time of a loss, it is often difficult to see a way forward, never mind think about the future, but somehow, we do find the stoicism and the resilience to get through those dark days.

When you sit and look at your timeline, rather than seeing it as the times which were difficult, think about them as times you faced difficulty yet you found the inner strength to find a way through adversity. Many people are often surprised by their level of resilience and stoicism after a loss, we don't often appreciate how strong we really are until we look back and realise what we have achieved.

My next story is a lady called Maggie. I sat with Maggie after she had completed a loss timeline and we talked about how she felt about the losses she had noted. Maggie's experience of her own loss had some long-lasting effects for her emotionally. At the time of one loss in particular, she had found it difficult to understand and find a way through the trauma she was experiencing, yet her story has a wonderful ending and one which gives hope to anyone who feels overwhelmed after a loss.

"Upon reflection after doing my own timeline of loss, one particular one seemed to feel quite poignant to me and upon spending some time thinking about it, it was one which resulted in me feeling quite emotional. I realised that this loss had had a profound effect on me as a person and that to this day continues to be part of my personality and the way I think and react in my current life.

My loss was in relation to a series of events which ultimately resulted in me losing my self-confidence and significantly lowering my self-worth for a long time. Many people may not consider this situation to be a loss but I have realised that they were events which irreversibly changed me, giving me a different outlook on life and although it didn't feel like it at the time, it actually made me a better person.

Several years ago, I was working in a job which I truly enjoyed, I loved going to work each day and I worked with an exceptional team of colleagues. It was a busy job and expectations were incredibly high nevertheless we made a difference to the people we supported and that to me was worth the long hours and the busy workload.

After a period of change within the organisation, the management structure was reformed and with those adjustments my job responsibilities dramatically changed too. Over a period of weeks and months I worked in my new role, however, I soon became less enthusiastic about the job and my overall experience of the new way of working. My diligence and commitment meant that I always gave 100% commitment. I felt I was consistently professional, and I always maintained a smile every single day, despite often being in tears on the way to work and on the way home from work, pretty much every single day. Then, one day with no notice, I received a call from management, I was to be made redundant.

The feelings of loss were overwhelming, the feelings were physical as well as emotional as I struggled to comprehend the news I had received. Why had I not been good enough? I was obviously a failure, as they didn't need me anymore. What had I done so wrong for them to do this to me? That day, after the call I remember leaving the office, feeling numb, I was innately logical and I understood what I had been told but at the same time I was in shock, I wanted to cry, I wanted to shout, I wanted to talk to someone but physically I could not talk, as I had lost my ability to speak. The loss of the job I had once enjoyed felt overwhelming.

Throughout those next few days, I started to rationalise the loss a little more and started to think more judiciously about the practicalities of the news. After a week, I left the company but I cried all day, and for the whole journey home on that last day.

My loss was not a bereavement, but it felt like grief and in essence I was indeed grieving but for the loss of my professional identity, the job I loved and the loss of all my colleagues who were at that point also my friends. I could not see past the 'loss', so I found it difficult to imagine life beyond those feelings, I couldn't imagine ever loving a job as much as I did that one and I missed the camaraderie of my work family and the relationships that had been built over time.

Thankfully, I was lucky to find another job quite quickly and it turned out to be a job I enjoyed immensely. I met a wonderful team of new colleagues and over time I found a meaningful purpose to life again as I started to grow in my new role and expand on new friendships.

It was a couple of years later that the effects of my experience started to play on my mind, as if they had left a lasting emotional scar. Despite loving my new role, I realised that I was struggling with my inner self-confidence and that I always had a sense of feeling 'paranoid' about my future. These feelings started to manifest into my life and work, and I started to think that my new team would see me as a failure if I made a mistake and I would lose my job again.

Several counselling sessions later, including extra EMDR (Eye Movement Desensitization and Reprocessing) sessions and I could finally say two very important sentences. "I am good enough" and "I am not a failure". It took a long, long time for me to say those words and truly believe them".

This story is poignant for so many reasons but mostly because it illustrates that loss can be traumatic too, it can be upsetting and difficult and it can sometimes be life changing, just like a bereavement. Maggie is in such a great job now and is incredibly happy and confident. Whilst life isn't always perfect, her self-esteem and self-worth have allowed her to regain her confidence again and look forward to a positive future.

4

Love, Loss, and Relationships

From very early on in our lives, we begin to learn some vital life lessons, one of those being the feelings associated with emotions, and how those emotions are important in relationships.

At a very young age, through our various social interactions we learn the importance of friendship and love. Do you remember that first childhood sweetheart? Maybe you used to hold hands in a school playground or share some sweets when the teachers were not looking? Life seemed beautifully simple during those times, but it was the start of an emotional journey, which as we grow older allows us to process those complicated emotions, and invest in our future relationships with a sense of anticipated confidence.

As humans we inherently seek companionship, the thought of 'love' and being in a relationship for many is integral to our envisaged futures, nonetheless it can be a journey which is both heart-warming and heart-breaking for so many different reasons. Whilst we all remember the love we share; it is the feelings of loss after a relationship which can linger in our memories, it can be incredibly powerful on a lasting emotional level.

As adults, we can often look back at our own memories and the times of heart-break, and we remember the rawness of the emotions we went through. At that time, we always thought the future was a dark place, and that we would never love again, life as we knew it was over, in our opinion! Of course, looking back now we know that wasn't true, but those feelings were real to you and anyone who has experienced them too will know that they can be exceptionally painful, and your heart feels shattered and broken at the time.

After a relationship breaks down, the associated distress can often be a sense of underlying anxiety, abandonment, and fears of being alone. Those overwhelming feelings are compounded by the perceived loss of our emotional security, and maybe even the simple fear of the unknown for the future.

What if however, we were to respond to those negative feelings in a positive way? Can we nurture those emotions to allow us to move on and to find happiness again? If we can find a way to mend our broken hearts, it must start with processing our own way of thinking.

In life, we cannot control what other people think or do, but we can control what 'we' say and do. If we pay attention to how we think about a loss we can start to process how we can incorporate a new way of thinking. When we try to understand that we cannot change some aspects of life, we can start to focus on the things we can change for the better.

As humans we are psychologically adept to dealing with bereavement, loss and grief, even though we have no control over when we experience them, nor can we stop them from happening. What we can do though is that when they do happen, we allow ourselves to be fully immersed in the emotions, even though they are painful and overwhelming. Recognising the reactions in the raw form that they are, allows us to develop the strength to enable us to grow around our bereavement or loss, and find a meaningful way forward. It is difficult and its certainly not easy, nonetheless it is an important step forward in our journey.

From those innocent childhood sweetheart moments, we all grow, and we develop a sense of resilience in our new relationships, across our lifetime. We form new partnerships, and new emotional bonds, which we nurture as we move forward in our daily lives. If we are lucky, those relationships may result in long-term commitments and/or marriage with many years of happiness.

As part of my working role, I am often privileged to speak with people who have been in relationships for upwards of 60-70 years, their stories are both inspiring and heart-warming as they share their memories with me, and try to pass on their secrets of a good relationship, which I always pay attention to! Despite grief being so painful when someone we love dies, especially after so many years together, the memories of that love and the many years of happiness are valuable in so many ways. Grief is the price we pay for our love yet that love is what gave us a lifetime of priceless memories.

Sadly, there are stories where those memories are maybe not as happy, with an example of this, being a break-down of a relationship. A relationship ending can lead to a person feeling an indescribable sense of loss, and to a certain extent grief. The loss of a relationship can be as traumatic as a bereavement in many ways. On an emotional level you are grieving the loss of the person you loved even though they are very much still alive.

Like grief, there is no right or wrong way to feel after the loss of a relationship, it is unique, and subject to individual circumstances. To understand this further, next is a story which gives a unique insight into the emotions experienced when a relationship ends.

Becky is in her early fifties, she married Will when she was nineteen. She had two children with her husband, however they divorced when she was in her mid-thirties. Her story is one which encapsulates how even though a loss feels unrecoverable, it is possible to find happiness again.

"When I married Will, I thought my life was mapped out, although I was young, I was happy, I wanted to start a family, and just enjoy life. I had been to college and wanted to work in a business role, although up to that point I had not really thought about an actual career, I was too busy being in love and planning a wedding.

After the wedding, we were happy for a while, but after the children arrived life seemed less exciting. I spent my days happily with the children which I loved, but the days were long, and I became increasingly eager to maybe go back to work. I eventually did find a job working in an office during school hours which I did enjoy, although if I'm honest, it wasn't my dream job.

It was a couple of years later when I started to notice my husband going out more, and becoming more and more distant. Not wanting to end the relationship I turned a blind eye and I acted as if I was fine. Life was not always a bed of roses, but my family meant everything to me so I chose to ignore the obvious.

It was summertime one year, when I found out by chance, that Will had been seeing someone from his work and he had been in the relationship with this person for a number of years. He admitted the affair to me straight away, and said he was moving out.

It is hard to truly put into words how I felt. I had known for such a long time that things weren't right, but at the same time when I heard the awful truth it was like someone punching me hard in the stomach. I felt so many emotions all at once that sometimes I couldn't even cry, it was difficult to comprehend how my life had come to that point. I was grieving the loss of my husband, my financial security, and my family life. When I sat down to really think about everything, I realised that despite all of the loss, at the heart of all that was also my own fear. I feared being all alone, and I was scared of losing the life I had spent so many years immersed in.

Over the months which followed, I had to find a way of starting my life again, which at times felt impossible. I was still in contact with Will as he maintained he wanted to keep up contact with our children, this however, was incredibly hard. Every time he came round to the house was like starting again, I felt so many feelings. One minute I was happy to see him, the next I wanted to punch him, then I would feel sad, but then equally I would be proud of how I was coping without him. Keeping that contact up with a stoic attitude was hard work.

It took me a long time to find the strength to become the confident person I am today. After the divorce, the losses felt as if they would never end, it was difficult to think how I would even begin to take a step forward.

I did take those brave steps though, and I am happy to say that the dark times did indeed pass. I found a great counsellor who helped me work through all my fears. More importantly, I learnt to like myself again as I developed a new sense of empowerment and self-confidence. With my new found confidence I started to go out again with my friends, which is when I met Tony. After a few months dating, we fell in love. Two years later we were married in a small ceremony surrounded by all our children, family and friends. My losses were many, yet my life now feels so enriched. I wouldn't change a thing; I was meant to be who I am now and, in the life, I am happily living."

The loss of a relationship can be life-changing, but as Becky's story illustrates, those losses have ripple effects across a person's life, so one loss inadvertently leads to another. However, what this story also shows is that despite those losses, with good support and time, it is possible to find a way through that uncertainty to find a meaningful and beautiful future.

5

Health Loss

My next case story is associated with a loss but the story itself is incredibly emotive and written so honestly by the person in respect of a loss. The loss at first seemed insurmountable, but in time ended up being life-changing for so many happy reasons.

Emma is in her 30's and at the start of her story she was a healthy, fun-loving woman whose life was full of adventure and enthusiasm. What happened to Emma came without any real warning, but it changed her life forever, however, through a great deal of tenacity, self-believe and sheer determination, Emma is now healthy, happy and back to living life to the full. This is Emma's story in her own words.

"My loss is not one which most people would expect, it is not even one loss but four, all different, but all connected. The loss of myself as a person, the loss of time, the loss of my health and the loss of life's adventures.

Being diagnosed with an illness at the age of thirty in 2014 was something completely unexpected. At the time I was a young excitable thirty-year-old woman who planned to travel, around the world to places such as Thailand, Australia, and Peru. I wanted to make that year one of my best celebratory life years, with all my friends and family, I also hoped to fully commit to my partner at the time, the love of my life.

Instead, it was the year I dealt with one of the scariest and often life limiting illnesses you can imagine, the terrifying illness, Cancer.

Upon finding a lump in my breast, I asked my mum to check it for me, I didn't want her to feel it, but I needed to know if I was just being paranoid. I remember the day clearly as it was her birthday. She agreed I should get it checked by the doctor so I made an appointment.

Little did we know just a month later the consultant would be saying, "it's not good news". I didn't know what he meant at first and I just needed him to say the words, 'Cancer'. When he said them, I burst into tears and repeated, "I knew it, I knew it".

After the diagnosis I felt weak, I lost weight and I felt so cold all the time. Life as I knew it was on hold, the wait when you think you have cancer is so long, I'd say one of the worst parts. You don't know if it's incurable. What's going to happen. People think you don't have it but deep down I could tell I was ill and that something was wrong, and I needed to be sure. During the wait and afterwards you feel like you can't make any plans and you feel lost and weary.

When I left the Consultant appointment, I left there with my friend and called my mum. I told her I'd be strong, and we'd be ok and I held my tears. I wanted to be strong for her. I wanted her to not be upset or worry. I remember saying "it's not great news, but don't worry I'll be fine, and I will get through this". My mum had previously lost her mum to cancer and I didn't want her to hurt or think she was going to lose her daughter too. I wanted her to not be upset because I cared too much about her to be the cause of her pain. I wanted her to know I would be okay. Previously she had also seen her brother go through bowel, liver, and testicular cancer. She had watched so many people suffer and just didn't want her to go through any harder times.

When the surgery plan was discussed, it was radical with the Doctors booking me in for a one-sided skin sparing mastectomy, they'd have to take everything from inside the breast including the nipple as I had five affected areas in total. I kept one breast hoping that if I had a child in the future, I would be able to breast feed.

Throughout the whole journey up to that point there was no question of dying I was going to fight it. After the mastectomy, I had wonky boobs and they were mismatched, I felt scared, sad, and so tense about what it was going to look like. For a few days after the surgery, I had a blood bag draining excess blood from inside. When I was discharged from hospital, they gave me a few weeks to recover, but then they started to talk about chemotherapy and radiotherapy.

During the follow up appointments the next cause of action was discussed and I was told the cancer had started to metastasise which meant there was probably more cancer ready to spread. Chemotherapy would kill any remaining or potential cells that wanted to breed; however, my cancer was oestrogen and progesterone positive (8/8) which meant it would feed off my own hormones. It was explained to me that the chemotherapy would obliterate my hormone receptive cells but by doing that it would also result in hair loss and receding gums.

It was at that time that they sent me to a fertility clinic to see if they could freeze some eggs to protect them, but the blowing news came that this would delay chemotherapy and that it wouldn't be safe for me. The egg freezing could if anything speed up any cell spread. Hearing that news, my heart sank; my friends were all having children and becoming families and now the chance to have a family of my own was being stripped away. I remember thinking how I would never make my mum a grandma, however I tried to keep focus on the fact that the important thing was to go through it all so I could live.

During the treatment, friends didn't know what to say to me, some friends I lost, and some friends became closer, some of my family were angry and could only express that emotion by being angry at me and then keeping their distance. This in particular hurt me in so many ways. I wondered how many other people also go through something like this too as it can be really hard to know how to feel about all the changes.

One particular experience was so hard for me, I was in a relatively good frame of mind on one particular day as I knew I had some more scans booked in and I was also seeing my consultant, and although the scans were scary, having answers always seemed to make me feel more in control. Someone was visiting me, however I felt as if they just didn't understand what I was going through and when I tried to explain I was quite directly told I was 'being selfish'. This hurt more than I let on, but I stayed calm and was rational, however that night following an argument with them I went to bed crying, feeling incredibly hurt. I saw that person only once when I was having my cancer treatment, I wanted them to see me with my bald head so that they could see what I was going through, however I was told to 'get a grip'. Sadly, that person truly didn't understand the suffering I was going through but I still forgave them as deep down I still loved them and knew that maybe they just didn't know how to cope with the fact I was so ill, but I still remember how that felt. The cancer was affecting my body, but it affects so many other areas of your life too.

There were so many physical changes I was going through, I was experiencing hair loss, constant throwing up, feeling bloated and my whole body just ached and was so tired. However, it was the loneliness which really stood out for me, at night I would be alone, it was just me and my kitten watching me as I was sick. At that time, despite all the physical and emotional problems, it was the not knowing if everything we were medically doing was getting rid of cancer, that was hard. I had no way of knowing if all of the pain and the suffering would be worth it.

At the time, I had a partner and I wondered how he could love me while I looked like an alien, he said he loved me, but he then went back to his ex, there was just too much tension and strain. I think in relationships people should be patient with the person with cancer and they should be extra sensitive with words or joking around especially when someone just needs either the space to process what is going on or simply just needs a comforting hug and to feel loved. There were a few instances where instead of knowing I had someone there to care for me and love me, I was left crying as I had been left alone, while they either went out socialising or they were too busy with other things. I was fighting cancer, I needed commitment, stability, and real love with someone who understood I was in an emotional mess.

It makes you see who is truly committed, you realise time is precious when others don't. I realise now that I stayed with him because I knew my love was true, but it just wasn't going to work in the long run. I realised in the end I deserved better.

I got through the treatment by showing people who followed me on Facebook I was strong, by being positive and showing my happy self. I think positivity helps to heal the mind and body, with endorphins, the positive chemicals running round your body. I also know that if it's 'your time' then no positivity will take away the pain and ending, memories are so important, having them and making them.

I never knew how many people cared about me till I posted that I had cancer on Facebook and people followed my journey. I've never been a confident person and always wondered if people liked me, but I've never been shown so much love, I received many wonderful messages and gifts. People need to continue that love through someone's journey as it is a massive support, it helps more than I can put into words.

People would then tell me if they were worried about a lump and that they would get checked, they realised if it had happened to me it could happen to anyone, and early diagnosis is so important. I'm so appreciative of all of the love shared. I believe so much in love and care.

When I was feeling a little better, I would make sure every week after chemotherapy me and my mum would go to Brighton or the Theatre, something unique and special. Our little trips out added a lot of happiness to the year, it meant that the year wasn't just about my fight to survive, it was about me trying to live my life still.

Getting through the treatment was hard but I met and was supported by an amazing MacMillan nurse who offered me both practical and emotional support throughout my journey, their help was invaluable. My amazing friends who had stayed by my side were always there to make me smile but mostly my mum who was my rock and still is. After my chemotherapy and radiotherapy treatment had finished, we celebrated with a party at my house and we went to see the Fireworks at St Albans, it was in-deed a time to celebrate, be grateful and be happy.

Having reached the end of the invasive treatment, I soon realised that it wasn't the end. Over the course of the year, it had been a fight just knowing which appointments I needed to attend so when I finished treatment and got the all clear in the November, I learnt that a new journey was about to start.

As part of my follow up treatment and part of the prevention plan, I was advised that I needed to take Tamoxifen and/or Zoladex and Exemestetane, these were hormone restricting drugs and would need to be taken for the next ten years. The medication would put me into early menopause at just thirty-one years old. I didn't know the impact of the menopause till it started happening and hated the brain fog and achy bones. I wanted to feel young, happy, and normal like everyone else.

At that time my hair was starting to grow back albeit in wispy patches, however I learned a little trick which was to highlight in the gaps with eye shadow which seemed to work well. I had gone from having long blonde hair to dark and patchy hair growing back which made me feel masculine and ugly.

In the weeks and months after treatment, I cried every morning, longing for the girl I used to be. People would ask me why I was upset and crying and would then say 'how lucky I was' and that 'I should be happy' but I had no idea what life from then on looked like and if my old life would ever come back. I was aching from the drugs and I felt like a shell of a person from the year that had passed. I had so many questions. What happened next? Would it come back? Would I be able to date with wonky boobs, my short hair and my bloated body from all the steroids?

People didn't understand, they wanted me to get 'back to normal'. I had no idea what that looked like anymore, I essentially had Post-Traumatic-Stress. It made me upset as I'd been as upbeat as I could yet that still wasn't enough for them. Some didn't want me to mention cancer ever again, but they didn't understand it wasn't over for me. I didn't know if it would come back, and it was scary. It takes time to get over a loss like mine however I feel that grief will always be there, it's just that over time it lessens. We evolve all the time through negative and positive experiences. I don't think there is just a thing as 'normal'. I hope with time we get stronger, more comfortable with ourselves and life experiences and that we can believe in our mind and body more, or at least I hope we all can. I hope when I'm old I can look back and be proud, that I lived the best I could.

Thankfully my MacMillan Nurse arranged for me to see a Counsellor from the hospice to help me with all my changing emotions. It was an elderly gentleman who I initially didn't think I would relate to but one session he asked me why I was upset for crying each day and how would I feel if a friend cried when looking back on that year. I realised I was being too hard on myself, I realised that I was actually allowed to be sad and that I was allowed to grieve for the me I had lost. It was from that session that the tears stopped and I started to feel strong again.

Looking forward from that point, I started dating an amazing guy who I was with for two years however, the hormone drugs played havoc with my emotions and when we were due to move up north, I cried so much I think it scared him away.

After four years of taking all the various drugs to help prevent the Cancer from returning, I took some time out and stopped taking them. For the first time in years, I felt less emotional, I felt more like me, my lust for life came back strong but, deep down I was scared of the cancer coming back, so I went back on them. I no longer had monthly periods, so I knew after the discussions at the hospital that I'd have no children and I felt that I had to deal with that on my own. I had to just get over it forget it and love my dog and cat like they were my babies.

At the end of 2020 I'd had enough of the drugs again, it had been six years and I felt like I had the bones of an eighty-year-old, I wanted to feel young again and wanted to know what my body and mind felt like without any hormone restricting drugs. Without them it made me feel great. The Oncologist agreed quality of life is important and I had done enough to help my risk or recurrence reduce.

Throughout my journey I always tried to remain super positive, I was especially happy when I managed my dreams to travel to Thailand and Peru on my own and then did Venice, Rome, Budapest, Vienna, Scotland, and Wales with my Mum. We made incredible memories to treasure with more to be made in the future.

A few months after, my hair grew for my best friend's wedding, I watched the world around me and watched my friends grow. My confidence returned and I was just happy being weird and quirky me. I felt that I was at the age where I was just happy being me, however there was still one thing missing, my own family.

In 2021 a miracle happened, despite all of the chemotherapy, hormone drugs, radiotherapy and all the scans, one strong little egg made it through all the treatment, and I found out I was pregnant.

My beautiful baby girl entered the world in 2021, she was and is perfect. I'd always wondered what my life had been missing and she was it, she brings me so much happiness that I cannot put into words how lucky I feel. I can only thank positivity, friends, family, and faith in believing that what is meant to be, will be and for always being there for me. We are all dealt a pack of cards in life, and we must play with the cards we are given. It's part of our unique and wonderful life experience, which includes the highs and the lows."

Emma's story is more common than you think, there are so many people going through the same type of loss and feeling all of those emotions which Emma talks about. Her experience of loss is one which is not associated with a physical loss of something around her, but of the loss of her physiological health, her mental health, and the consequences of both on the world around her. Her stoicism and bravery are simply outstanding with her positive attitude to her changing world being inspirational.

When providing the dialogue for her story, Emma found it quite hard at first and she commented on how it was hard to talk about all the feelings and emotions she had been through, however at the end she also commented on how cathartic it had been and that when she re-read her words, she realised how far she had come, and how proud she was of how she coped.

"You forget how hard it was and I've never been one to dwell so seeing it written down I don't give myself credit for keeping so strong. I've been through hard times and just feel so lucky now, I love how my story ends with all the good things that have happened, so if anything, I'd like to give people hope "

6

Grief and Mourning

Grief and mourning are very personal experiences and as such come with intense feelings and thoughts about bereavement. Grief put simply is how those personal feelings of loss are internalised and experienced.

Mourning is when the internalised grief is projected outwards, it is the process that occurs after a bereavement and is often referred to as the process which allows us to accept loss and adapt to life without a loved one.

Grief can encompass many feelings such as sadness, anger and disbelief which may also be accompanied by physical symptoms such as stomach pains, headaches, sickness, and insomnia. Changes in behaviour both physically and cognitively are common with memory loss and changes in concentration being affected. These are all normal reactions and part of the grieving process. However, they are often feelings which are kept private by most of us during such a difficult time.

In the early stages of grief, it is often hard to 'find the words' and to find any meaning to a bereavement and therefore the grief is at first internalised. In contrast, mourning occurs when that emotion is shown outwardly, for example when we display feelings of anger about the loss or if we cry in front of others.

Mourning may include some or all the reactions associated with grief, however they are more outwardly visible. Mourning can be a long and painful process, but it is a normal and healthy part of the grief journey. It can help us to remember our loved ones and to allow us to slowly process and adapt to a new way of living. In time we start to live alongside our grief in our daily life, and even allow ourselves to feel happiness and enjoyment again.

After a bereavement, how many times have you heard the sentence “It will take some time, but you'll get back to normal” or “life will get back to normal soon”, these are just two of the many different ways of trying to say that after a bereavement life goes ‘back to normal’. I wish I could say that was true, but sadly it is far from the truth. Every bereavement changes us, it could be in a small way, or it could be life-changing, either way I don't think we ever really ‘go back to normal, instead we adapt to a new way of life, maybe even calling it the ‘new normal’.

For me personally, my life after 2019 was anything but normal, my life changed in every aspect. It changed my way of thinking, and it changed the way I live, in fact, it touched every single part of my life, in differing ways.

When Jay was given his terminal diagnosis, I knew that life as I had known it was about to irreversibly change, at the time I could only hypothesise about what it would be like and how it would feel but in reality, it was beyond what I could have imagined.

My ‘normal’ life prior to his illness and his death was what you would consider to be pretty ordinary. We had not long brought a house together, we both worked full-time jobs, we paid our bills, but never really had that much extra, nonetheless we always made sure our boys never went without so we still enjoyed holidays and trips out and maybe a few too many meals out in the evenings. Life wasn't always great but it certainly was never bad, we were happy and content with what life had given us. Of course, all that changed after Jay's death.

Hearing someone say 'Life will get back to normal soon' after someone dies can feel wrong and you can feel a range of different emotions. You may feel angry at people for thinking you could just get over someone's death. How it is even remotely possible to get over such a loss straight away? Within your own circle of grief, it can feel like no one else is feeling the pain you are feeling. Many people say that when that they lose someone close to them, they feel that their 'world stops turning' and that they lost a part of themselves when that person died. It is those initial thoughts and feelings which make grief so overwhelming in the beginning. 'Normal' life is definitely not something you can contemplate at that moment in time.

Following a conversation with my sons about the use of the word 'normal' after a bereavement, I asked what they thought, and their response was incredibly thought-provoking. My youngest son said, "I don't really know how to explain it, but it's the same feelings as when someone says 'oh just cheer up' or 'be happy', it feels insensitive, but maybe it's a lack of understanding. How can you go back to normal when that person can't come back?".

Losing someone you love or care about is emotionally overwhelming and there is no time limit as to how long the grieving and mourning process takes. I often talk about this experience as a metaphor;

"Imagine you are carrying your grief in several heavy buckets, at first, they feel heavy, and you feel as if you cannot carry on as you feel weighed down and tired. Over time, you grow a little bit stronger, it does not happen overnight, it could take weeks, months or even years. One day you realise that the buckets have the same amount of grief in them but they feel a little lighter and less overwhelming. Do you sometimes need to stop and take a break? Absolutely. Will there be times when they feel heavier than usual? Definitely. The moral of the story is that grief does get easier over time, however the grief doesn't actually leave you, we just learn to adapt to having it in our lives, we grow stronger around our grief so that we can carry on and find a meaningful way forward"

7

Unresolved Grief

After a bereavement there are so many prominent feelings and thoughts. They often leave a person feeling overcome with a sense of uncertainty about how to take those first steps forward in the 'new-normal' world they find themselves in.

It was following a conversation with an acquaintance that I found myself thinking about my own grief. We had a very honest conversation about our grief, talking about how we had coped in those early days, and how it made us feel.

Whilst grief is unique and a very individual journey, often you may find that you can identify with some of the emotions or actions others have experienced, and you can relate their journey to yours. Many people find being able to relate to someone else comforting, and whilst we are all different it can be nice to share that commonality.

My next story is a lady called Tina; she is a truly remarkable lady. Tina was married to her husband Tom for many years, they lived happily in a house they had resided in for over thirty years and shared their life together in a sense of unbridled happiness, until one day life as they knew it changed.

"When Tom died, I felt very lost. Initially I was in shock, I couldn't talk at first, I just didn't have any words to say. Tom had been diagnosed with cancer just over three years ago, whilst he was at times quite poorly, the cancer was being managed successfully, and he was in good health overall.

When Tom died, it happened so fast, one minute he was okay, but a day later he was gone. I feel like I lost my memory that day as there are parts of the day, I still to this day cannot remember anything about what I did. I know people were around me, but I was oblivious to them.

After the funeral, there was so much to do. I was trying to sort out all the house paperwork, but I had no idea what I was doing. In the end my son helped me. Money was a problem though; Tom was the only person who worked as I had given up work due to a medical condition. I was so stressed, I didn't know how I could afford the house, the car or how I would afford the lifestyle I was used to.

It was a couple of months before I started to receive letters back from all the companies about Tom's financial matters. He had a pension and life insurance so those were in the process of being paid to me. I felt so guilty when I received the money, it felt wrong. What made it worse was that despite my initial worries, I then had more money than we had before, so the feelings of guilt made me worse. I didn't want the money, yet I needed it to be able to continue living in the house.

I remember, it was about four months after Tom died, I had to complete a form for something to do with the house, and I had to put myself down as a 'Widow'. I hated it, I cried the whole day. It felt so unfair.

My friends were lovely and rallied round me, I can't deny that they were all really good, even though all I wanted to do was shut myself in the house, and never go out. They kept on asking me to go out for a coffee or a 'spot of lunch.' I know it was from a place of kindness, but they are all married, they are happy and I couldn't admit to them that I felt left out.

I used to go to church with Tom, although I admit not every Sunday, nevertheless we tried to go as much as we could, Tom's work allowing. Nowadays I can't bring myself to go. I'm still really angry that he died, I feel like I have no reason to be thankful or to be grateful. I don't understand why he was taken from me. Maybe that will change one day, in fact I'm sure it will, just not right now.

My family and friends tell me that I'm 'doing okay', but that's because I never cry in front of them, I put on a brave face, I try to convince them I'm alright. I hate that I hide it from them, but I just cannot bring myself to tell them how I really feel. I just need to keep going. When I stop, I start to think about Tom, it upsets me. I then spend the rest of that day not being able to do anything. I'm not ignoring the fact I'm sad, I just don't know how to see a way through it all at the moment."

Tina's words are very emotive, and at the time of writing this, the emotions around her bereavement were unresolved and still very painful for her. Thankfully after Tina shared her story with me, she spoke to me about how she found writing her emotions and thoughts down. Whilst, it was difficult, it was also cathartic for Tina as it was the first time, she had really expressed how she was feeling. Tina later went on to seek professional bereavement counselling, which is helping her to process all her difficult emotions, helping her find a meaningful way through her grief.

Writing is an excellent way of processing our emotions, especially difficult emotions such as grief. Writing allows you to put into words what may be difficult to say out loud. It may be that you wish to express an anger about a situation or just feel like you need to share your thoughts to rationalise them.

Expressive writing has been shown to reduce anxiety and depression as well as promoting good general mental health and wellbeing as it allows you to really 'feel' the emotions associated with grief and bereavement, and to start to work through them over time.

All you need to do, is take a pen and paper, or a laptop, and start writing. Think about how you *really* feel. Remember you don't need to worry about upsetting anybody so really write about what emotions or feelings that you have.

In words, you can tell the person who has died, how you really feel, maybe tell them something you wish you had said, or maybe just tell them what's going on your life right now, there really is no right or wrong way to write about your feelings, as long as it helps you.

An example of some excerpts from letters could be:

"Dearest Dad, I'm really sorry that I never got to tell you that I loved you, I was always so busy with work. I do love you though, I always have and always will. I miss you so much"

"I smiled today, and I thought of you. I felt guilty for smiling at first, but I know you would be so proud of me and your children for staying strong. We miss you so much."

"I am angry with you for leaving me"

"I feel really sad today, I just want to cry all the time. I know you would have stayed if you had the choice. Someone asked me today if I'm okay, I said yes. What I actually wanted to say is that my heart is breaking, no I'm not okay."

This is an incredibly powerful exercise to do and one which can re-visited as many times as you feel is helpful. Remember these letters are private and meant to be read by only you. Keep your letters safe and out of view or you can write the letter and then destroy it. This exercise is more about releasing those inner emotions and allowing yourself to externalise your thoughts and feelings.

8

Multiple Bereavements

The experience of one grief is incredibly difficult, but when there are multiple bereavements, the grieving process may take longer or feel more complicated as you try to process multiple feelings about the losses.

In my next case story, we meet a gentleman who found himself grieving for not just the loss of his baby daughter but his mother and wife too. His story is incredibly moving and one which really touched me emotionally as he eloquently conveys his experience and how it affected his life both historically, and to the present day.

James is in his sixties; he lives with his Husband John in their dream house in the countryside. James has sadly experienced many bereavements in his life, including his ten-month-old daughter, his late-wife Dawn, and his mother.

James's story is incredibly moving but what makes his story special is that I have also included the words and experiences from Dawn too. Prior to her death in 1996, she wrote a short story of her cancer diagnosis which I was privileged to read alongside James's story. Her words are very emotional and really capture the journey they both went through. James was happy for them to be intertwined within his story.

"In 1979, my life changed forever, when my beautiful baby daughter, died of 'cot death', aged only ten months old. On that day me and her mother had an argument, sadly that argument was to be one I would always remember. That night her mother put my daughter to bed without bringing her to me for a goodnight kiss, I guess most of the time this would go un-noticed but not having that last kiss is upsetting to me even to this day, as it was to be the last opportunity, I would get to kiss her beautiful face, and wish her sweet dreams.

My daughter had always been healthy and for her to die so suddenly it had a dreadful effect on me and it played on my mind for an incredibly long time. At the time, I was a young dad of only 22-years-old and although I went on to have other children, my daughter was my first-born so she holds a special place in my heart.

Sadly, our marriage did not last, it was certainly not the only reason we separated but it was losing our daughter and her affair which resulted in our divorce and yes, I did hold a grudge for many years against her for the loss of that special goodnight kiss.

Following our divorce, I was left to raise our children. I found this really difficult so I eventually moved to be closer to my parents who were a great support to me.

I decided to look for group support and found Birmingham Gingerbread, an association for one parent families. I became a very active member of that group, and it was during that time that I met Dawn who was the secretary of the group.

Dawn had one son and was a one-parent family like myself. Weeks and months went by as Dawn and I grew closer and we made the decision to move in together. It was after that time that we both left Gingerbread, however it was with a heavy heart as it was always so special to me. After a year, life was changing for the better, we had moved into a new three-bed council house, Dawn had started her job as a school secretary, and I started a job for the local council. Life was good. If only we had known what was ahead of us.

In December 1992, we were dealt the devastating news that Dawn had cervical cancer, she was initially told it was terminal and that the prognosis was around six months, however that timescale would only be achieved if she underwent a complex and lengthy surgery with several different consultants involved. We were told by the Consultant that the percentage of her making it through the ten-hour operation was very low. Throughout the consultation we sat in the room taking all the information in, the consultant talked about the 'tumour' and his plans, however it was only when he said the word 'cancer' that Dawn's world fell apart and her face changed from worried to scared.

I remember driving home from the hospital that day, knowing that I had to drive to my elderly-in-laws to inform them that their daughter did not have long to live, it was by far one of the worst things I have ever had to do. I found myself trying to support three very upset adults, but I had to try and be the strong one. Dawn was inconsolable and cried the whole way back but I held her hand despite me driving, I didn't want to let go of her.

Dawn and I decided not to tell the children that they were about to lose their mother until it was necessary. It took a massive strain on me trying to explain why Dawn would be crying as I could offer them no reason.

After the initial shock, we decided that we both needed to grab every chance we had to live together for as long as possible as we had four children in the household who needed their mother for as long as possible.

The following weeks seem to be a blur, Dawn went back to work for a short while and seemed to want to keep herself busy, although it was clear that her illness was always at the forefront of her mind. The surgery date had been confirmed and as much as possible life carried on until the date finally came around, however we were both incredibly nervous and worried about what was going to happen and if the surgery would be successful.

The surgery went ahead, and it was thought to be a success, however, we were told that a few of the lymph nodes had been affected so radiotherapy treatment was required.

During that time, I was also supporting my own mother who was suffering from terminal colon cancer and was herself in a hospice. I remember the day after Dawn's discharge, she was adamant that she visited and accompanied her to one of her hospital appointments, even though she should have been at home resting, this was one of Dawn's many attributes, her kindness and compassion was extraordinary. Two weeks later sadly my mother passed away with myself and the family at her bed side.

Everything that was happening was showing effects on my mental health and I decided to take some time off work as Dawn's health was worsening, and I also had to arrange my mother's funeral. The expected two-week sick leave lasted over six months in the end.

After Dawn's surgery and my mother's funeral we tried to live life as best we could, we even booked a holiday to Cornwall one August, in fact it was after that holiday that we returned to a letter from the Consultant telling Dawn that the latest batch of tests were all clear of any cancer cells. The elations and the relief were beyond words and the thought of living life cancer free left both of us with a renewed sense of hope and positivity for the future.

Later that year, Dawn began to feel unwell again, so further tests were arranged. A week later we found out that the consultants secretary had been trying to contact us to ask us to go in to see him. Alarm bells rang and we were instantly worried as the consultant wanted to run further tests. The results came back and it was confirmed the cancer had spread and further surgery was needed, but it was incredibly complex and a further specialist's input was required.

The surgery required was indeed complex and physically life-changing, it was a massive decision and left us with more questions than we had answers. On the day of the surgery, I remember sitting with Dawn prior to the surgery trying to conceal my overwhelming sense of fear and uncertainty, her life was about to be placed in the hands of the surgeons and all I could do was wait.

The surgery went well, albeit with some complications but the recovery was harder than we expected, and we both struggled with our emotions. For a few more months Dawn recovered and we once again tried to live life as best we could, albeit it was hard at times.

In 1995, during a regular hospital visit Dawn found a small lump, at first the consultant wasn't too concerned; however, it was diagnosed as cancerous with local spread, so chemotherapy and radiotherapy was scheduled. After Dawn's second round of Chemotherapy, she was physically and mentally exhausted, she had also at that point found further lumps, in addition to the original lump. It was at that point that Dawn was told that the Chemotherapy wasn't working and that in their medical opinion it was best to stop treatment. The prognosis was six months.

Once Dawn had been diagnosed and after a few weeks without me knowing, she made sure that everything that was necessary for her passing was going to be put in place. Without me knowing, she had organised our finances to ensure that we would be okay after her death, she had even organised her own funeral with specific instructions, even down to the music choices. Although scared, she was incredibly courageous in her final weeks, she found the time and energy to write her memoir which is so beautifully written as it's all in her own words, however towards the end she became more tired and asked me to finish it for her, knowing that I had shared her journey with her.

In March 1996, Dawn was admitted to a hospice so she could receive round the clock care and support. This part of the journey was I suppose the most difficult for me. While I was sitting in the hospice and certainly in her final days, we had a conversation where she said, "whatever makes you happy in life, go out and find it". This was difficult for me because as much as I loved Dawn, I found that I was fighting my own sexuality and although it was never discussed as a conversation, it felt like she was giving me permission to accept who I was. I felt guilty for many years after that but eventually (three years later), I accepted my sexuality believing I had her approval.

Knowing she was eternally loved and with me by her side, in May 1996, Dawn sadly died. After Dawn had passed away, I didn't know what my future was going to hold or even if I had a future.

Throughout Dawn's illness and up to her death and funeral, I had received an abundance of support and help from my friends and family, however I felt so alone. After the funeral in particular I found people appeared to keep away as if they didn't know what to say to me, when in fact I didn't really need anyone to treat me any different, all I needed was someone to pass the time of day with or maybe ask me out for a coffee etc. Friends and family did come back into my life, probably about two-three months later when I think they thought my loss would not be as bad, unfortunately this is not true as there is no time limit on grieving and loss.

At the time I was still off work, all the caring had got on top of me and eventually I ended up having a breakdown. I started drinking more alcohol than I should and I couldn't seem to lift my mood. Thankfully, I did get some advice for the drinking and my mood which helped me to recover.

I did also attend a bereavement group at the hospice where my wife passed, I guess my thinking was that it would be good to be around like-minded people. Unfortunately, I didn't find it helpful as every time I went in there would be a new group member and we would have to explain to the new member what stage we were at in the bereavement process. For me, this felt like every week I had to relive my wife's death and instead of helping me it was making me worse. (I'm not saying counselling is bad for everyone, it just wasn't right for me).

In those first few weeks and months I do remember someone saying about 'going back to normal' after Dawn had died. I actually hate the term 'go back to normal', just as much as the phrase "you have to be positive". How can anyone know what 'my normal' is? My normal would be living without my loss, what happens after that is a 'new normal' but other people still wouldn't know my 'new normal'.

There is never a birthday or anniversary where my lost ones are not mentioned, in fact I often talk to my husband about my late daughter and late wife.

Myself and my husband now care for my late wife's mother, she is 99 and currently lives in a nursing home We visit twice a week and it's guaranteed that we all have a conversation of some kind about my late wife, but it is also nice to know that she has accepted my new future, she loves me as much as she ever did but she also loves my husband too.

Looking forward, my children all now have families of their own, something I am very proud of. I love my future now, I suppose I worry more about my health and that of my husband, but we have had a wonderful time since we met and done quite a lot of travelling which we enjoy. I am so pleased to say that I have got a future.

My advice to anyone going through a similar situation is simply to take care of yourself, don't worry if you cry as that is good for you. Don't wait for others to mention your loved one, bring up the conversation yourself, it will help them to realise that they can talk to you as it will help you and them.

Always remember the good times and the smiles will return, your future is ahead of you."

Before she died, Dawn wrote a beautiful poem for James and with his permission I would like to share it.

You wiped away my teardrops,
You eased away my pain,
You've shown me endless happiness,
You've helped me live again,
I liked you, now I love you,
I want you more each day,
I'll need your strength forever,
To guide me along the way,
So, darling please believe me,
When I say our love's divine,
Just let us both remember,
That I am yours and you are mine.

Written by Dawn (1955-1996)

James's story is one many people may resonate with; the ability to say goodbye or indeed not being able to say goodbye before someone dies can have a profound effect on how we grieve and how we deal with the bereavement in the long term. Thoughts such as 'I wish I could have...', 'I should have done ...' or 'If only I had...', are just a small handful of the questions and thoughts which we can have following a death. Although in time those questions get a little less intrusive, they never really leave us, we always have that thought process of wanting to know the truth about something or wishing we could change the past.

How many times have you heard the phrase "If I could turn back time" or "If I only knew then what I know now"? It is a hard realisation after a loss that we crave the normality of the life we had before, however it's an impossible quandary with no realistic answer. As we all know we cannot turn back time which plays heavy on both the heart and the mind.

James's story is one which I feel incredibly privileged to share, he has been through some truly upsetting experiences and has the emotional scars to prove it. His life now is surrounded by love, companionship and hope but he will never go 'back to normal', instead he embraces his 'new normal' and his new life with a renewed sense of optimism and resilience.

9

Field of Grief

Imagine, you are standing in a field, the grass around you is tall, the sun is shining and there isn't a cloud in the sky. You can hear birds singing and the rustle of the branches on the trees around you and in the distance the faint sounds of children happily playing. You can feel the warmth of the evening sun on your face but with a gentle breeze which takes away the summer heat. You take a deep breath in and let out all the stressors of your day, you close your eyes and take in all the senses around you. You feel a sense of serenity and peace, like the world you live in is somehow over the horizon and that life in that moment is perfect.

Some may say that this scenario is idyllic and perfectly serene and certainly somewhere you might want to be right now, I know it would be for me! For that one moment, life pauses and you can forget about everything around you, your thoughts, your worries, and your fears.

Then imagine, one day whilst you are standing in that field with life passing you by, you experience a sudden loss or bereavement. At first, your reaction might be denial, after all you are okay, you are perfectly happy in your beautiful field so it can't possibly be happening to you, it must not be real, but then slowly you realise it is real and it is happening.

A loss and/or bereavement can at first feel like someone has suddenly taken away all those wonderful feelings of warmth, tranquillity, and happiness. It can initially feel incredibly overwhelming and there may be a sense of not knowing how to respond, act or even talk. What was 'normal' is now the opposite of 'normal', the serene field you were standing in now feels very different, it almost feels colder and uninviting.

The circumstances of loss are individual to each and every person, but let's face it, we are not always standing in a beautiful relaxing field with life being tranquil. Sometimes life can be in a dark space already and then another loss comes along just to make life that little bit harder than it already was.

Looking back at the losses and bereavements across our lives, there have probably been many which have caused us great upset and immense sadness, however there are also a few which we have possibly been able to learn from and gain great insight from. All those times however, all have a profound effect on us and stay with us for a long time, if not forever.

A loss and/or grief is something which never truly leaves you as a person, it can sit harmlessly in the background of your life or it can be all-consuming and dominate everyday living, nonetheless it is part of who you are and it sits alongside the rest of life's journey.

For me personally, my 'serene field' now looks a little different to before. You can't go 'back to normal', as normal isn't there anymore, however the 'new-normal' adapts to changing circumstances. The field you once stood in is still sunny and warm, it still feels peaceful and is still a place of tranquillity, however it is also now a field with an area of reflection and a specific area which is dedicated to the loss or losses you have experienced.

When you stand in your 'field', you will know that the loss is there and occasionally you will walk over to sit there for a little while to reflect and think about the losses it represents. That area of the field is part of who you are and in time knowing that it is okay to visit that sadness and to reflect on those losses is important. It allows us to maintain a sense of feeling grounded and to acknowledge the loss, whilst at the same time finding the strength to sit beside it and not feel overwhelmed by its presence. It takes time, but it is possible.

10

Bereavement and Guilt

My next story is from 50-year-old, David. He experienced the death of his grandma quite a few years ago now, however the memories are still as poignant today as they were at the time of the bereavement. In his story although he talks about his grief over the death of his grandma, he also talks about the associated losses he felt in respect of his decisions before and after she died and how they have affected him to this present day.

"One of my closest relationships was with my Grandma Dorothy who sadly passed away in 1997. I remember the year quite vividly, I was twenty-four years old, just married and looking to start a family of my own.

I actually feel quite lucky as I have only experienced the loss of my grandparents and family pets up to now, however I found it strange at the time how the level and intensity of the bereavement changed dependent on the relationship I had with each of my grandparents as I thought it would feel the same. I also remember feeling that same sense of loss when I had to have my dog put to sleep. I found it strange how the loss felt different for each one.

Dorothy had been ill for a number of months after contracting pneumonia in the previous winter however despite being in hospital she did manage to return home. Unfortunately, despite initially being well enough to be discharged her health declined again and she was readmitted to hospital just before Christmas. During her stay in hospital, we were initially told to expect the worse as her health deteriorated, nevertheless she started to show signs of recovery and a few days later and just after Christmas I was able to visit her one morning in the hospital.

On that particular day, our family's football team were playing an important match and wanting to attend the game I managed to convince my father after visiting her that my grandma was well enough for us to attend, so that afternoon we travelled to the ground together to watch our team play. I was reassured that this decision was okay as my aunt had agreed to visit my grandma around lunchtime.

That afternoon, it appears as soon as my grandma had seen my auntie, she rapidly went downhill. We received the news that evening that she had passed away.

I felt incredibly guilty after hearing the news, I also felt so selfish for convincing my father that my grandma was well enough for us to attend the football match. I felt that I had deprived him of the opportunity to see her one last time and to say goodbye.

I refused the opportunity to visit my grandma in the following days, not because of the guilt but because I didn't want to see the fragile body of the grandma I loved so very much. I really don't hold any religious views; however, I do believe that the physical body of a person is the vessel for the soul and that her soul was now in the afterlife so if I visited it felt to me as if I wasn't really seeing her, it was just her body as her spirit and memory lived on in me.

For me the most difficult part was knowing she would not be in my life physically anymore, I missed her terribly which was hard to comprehend. At her funeral, I refused to throw dirt on the coffin and could not approach the grave, before or during the service.

I struggled to feel close to anyone during that period of time and I distanced myself from my grieving grandfather and the rest of the family. In my mind and for reasons I cannot explain I blamed them for not looking after her properly before she was poorly. My grandparents were from a different time and world, and it wasn't till later in life that I accepted the relationship and dynamic between my grandparents was appropriate for them. It was hard to even visit my grandfather after she died because of the house they lived in and seeing her chair empty.

Whilst I was trying to process my grief and to try to find some sort of acceptance for it all I had to remember that I was a newlywed and my wife was eager to start a family, but her eagerness was sadly untimely, and I found it hard to think about that whilst trying to grieve.

I had found the experience of seeing my grandma so ill upsetting and then her passing away incredibly stressful that although I was excited at the prospect of having my own family, it felt selfish and disrespectful to be contemplating such a happy occasion. Sadly, my wife was not understanding of this at the time, and this added to the stress I was already struggling with.

After my grandma died, my family had to sort out all the practical and legal elements and I remember being shocked at how that affected the family dynamics. The thought of gaining material objects and inheriting money certainly made some of the family members change their moralities and ethical values, I remember being quite shocked at how instead of the death bringing us closer together in fact it almost drove us all apart.

The expectation on myself as the eldest grandchild was that I should have been actively involved in the funeral however this was hard as I didn't want to say goodbye, I didn't want to put her physical form into the ground, I just wanted to say goodbye in my own way, which was remembering her for all her good points and valuing been able to see her on the morning of her death. Sadly, my family couldn't understand this, and I suspect an element of resentment was aimed my way for a period of time following her death due to my feelings. Many kept their distance as I think I disappointed them in not been more active in the funeral. To this day I still don't know how my father felt about us attending the football match, but I feel unable to ask him now time has elapsed.

Looking back, if support had been available to help me come to terms with the decisions I made, I'm not sure if I would have accepted it. I was twenty-four years old and the last thing I felt I needed at the time was emotional support as in my mind that was the first thing to potentially threaten my own sense of immortality. I know my father gained a lot of comfort from a visit by the vicar that was involved in the service, however due to my own personal beliefs I declined to participate in those meetings. I believe time and self-acceptance are great healers, I truly believe that there is no right or wrong time period for grief, as the actual physical grief for me only lasted twenty-four hours, however the emotional grief is still with me today. I still strive to do my grandma proud and truly hope that if religion is real heaven gained an angel on the day she died.

I am a big believer that time is the healer and at the moment my future looks good. I look back and I recognise that even during the bereavement I knew it was only a temporary feeling and that it would eventually become easier, after all 'it can't rain all the time', however, my journey is still ongoing. I miss my grandma so much and looking back now I would have loved to have spent more time with her and in the present, I would love to just sit with her and talk to her about my life. I do however still ask her for guidance, and I am still very mindful of how she would feel about the things I do and the decisions I make. The one positive outcome is that to this day I try to live to the values my grandma instilled in me, and I always aim to do her proud. My beautiful niece has since been named after my grandma, which I know she would have loved as well as it being great having her name back in the family.

When it comes to the anniversary's now, I just quietly note them, I think of her beautiful smile and how much I loved her and if I am local, I visit to place some flowers on the grave. She remains and will always be in my heart.

After a loss I would argue with the logic of being able to just 'get back to normal' after such a loss, normal is something which is individual and if someone had said that to me, I'm not sure if I would have been able to answer them as defining normal is too subjective."

David's story is poignant for so many reasons, however it does highlight the nature of grief and how even over many years, grief can evoke many emotions and feelings. The emotional impact around the nature of David's loss has shaped his life now and how he lives in the present. David's life now is one of much happiness, his life is blessed with love and prosperity, surrounded by his family and friends who love and support him.

On a day-to-day basis we make decisions and choices which at the time may feel insignificant or irrelevant, but it is those very decisions that can frame our future, especially when there is an unexpected loss. We cannot however pre-empt those losses and therefore we can only do our best to make the choices we feel are right at the time.

11

Unexpected Health Loss

Loss and bereavement are in essence just words, but they are words associated with a whole range of emotions, reactions, and feelings, for some they hold minimal significance, for others the thought of a specific loss or bereavement can trigger many difficult memories and/or thought processes.

For the next case story, I will be unexpectantly using my own experience, but it is not associated with my previous losses, it is a specific loss associated with something I have found quite difficult to talk about. In addition to my narrative, it will be followed by another perspective, my husband Gareth's. He shared that journey with me but experienced it differently to me so to really appreciate how loss is experienced it is interesting to hear the same story but with a different outlook.

"In March 2022, I attended a regular mammogram at my local hospital, it was a routine yearly follow up appointment as I was on an annual screening system. I attended the appointment as normal; everything went fine, and I was told the results would be posted out to me.

A few days later I had a call from the hospital, the lady on the phone calmy informed me that the results had shown something and I needed to go back for further tests. In that moment, my heart started beating faster but my world slowed and almost stopped. In an instance, my mind went blank as I realised that my world potentially had just changed and that from that moment, I had no idea what was going to happen to me. Human nature meant that I jumped to every negative assumption about the reasons for me being recalled, I was in shock, and I don't mind admitting, I was scared.

I sat down after the call and tried to comprehend what was happening and tried to find some level of emotional and rationality from it all. In that moment, I realised that my 'loss', was now the loss of control and the potential loss of my health, I was grieving for something I had no idea would even happen, yet I still felt like I had lost everything.

A couple of hours later I realised I needed to ask more questions about the call, as waiting for four days would be too much, so I rang the breast care unit to ask for more information. I was surprisingly calm on the phone until I was transferred to a Breast-Care Nurse. I explained the reason for my call, and she was so kind and offered to read the report to me. She explained that three specialists had looked at my report, one had said it was the same as the 2021 scan, one had said there were changes so a third specialist was consulted, who decided that I should be followed up as there were obvious subtle changes on the scans. Although it wasn't great news, it put my mind at rest a little as I knew they had found nothing obvious. Those four days however went incredibly slow, as all I could think about was 'what next?'

Losing your sense of normality can often feel quite traumatic, whether that loss be a bereavement or a loss of something important to you, it is still upsetting and it is still distressing. It is quite normal, to lose your sense of self, to feel lost and uncertain about what to do, and who to talk to.

On the contrary it could be that a loss can inspire a person to feel more motivated and to be full of positivity so they can proactively rise above the adversity.

Over the four days which followed, the waiting was incredibly hard, every hour felt twice as long and the more time I had, the more I ruminated about the possibilities, both good and bad.

From the start of this particular journey, I was incredibly lucky as I had my amazing ('to-be' at the time) husband by my side every step of the way, he was adamant I was going to be okay, yet at the same time he never once told me I was being silly or daft about my concerns, he was just simply there, which meant the world to me and was exactly what I wanted to hear.

On the day of the appointment, we arrived on time and made our way up to the hospital entrance, I felt nauseous, and the sense of trepidation was quite overwhelming. We checked in with reception and we sat down to wait for my name to be called. I remember there was a TV on in the waiting room and although the programmes being aired were beyond watchable, it seemed to help as it took our minds off the waiting. As I sat there, looking around the room, I made a fleeting look towards Gareth.

For the first time since we met, I could see actual fear in his eyes, I had never seen him look scared before so it served to amplify all our emotions, but strangely, I have never felt so close to him as in that moment I realised how much I needed him and how much I needed his support. I knew I could get through anything with him, holding me and being by my side.

When my name was called, I took a big breath and walked over to the nurse. We went into a clinical room and as I sat in front of the two nurses who explained the process to me and what to expect. They were so kind, their words were professional but also realistic, they told me the truth which I did prefer. Their words were comforting and made me feel reassured and I knew that irrespective of the outcome, I was in good hands. I went back through to the waiting room and awaited to be called in again for the various additional scans.

That wait was probably the worst part of the day as I managed to convince myself that the news would be bad and that the nurses were being nice because they knew the results already so they were preparing me for the eventual diagnosis of breast cancer.

Half an hour later after undergoing all the relevant test (although it felt like a lot longer!) I heard the words "it's okay, we can send you home". I remember saying 'pardon' and 'say that again' to the consultant, as I struggled to take in the news that I was in the clear. The kind nurse who stayed with me after the consultant left was incredible, she understood my tears and she let me have 'a moment' to gather myself and take in the good news.

I came out that room, went straight across to Gareth and just held him so tight. During that time, the feeling of loss was magnified not just due to the unknown but also the fact I had no control over the outcome of my results. Physically and metaphorically speaking I didn't lose anything that day so it could be argued that the experience could not be considered as a 'loss'. I certainly cannot give it a physical label like I would for example if I lost my phone or if I spoke about someone I had 'lost' from a bereavement however, it is a loss and it had a profound effect on me and my future.

That day was officially a good day, but it changed me, it made me realise that life is so precious and that everything I have been through to date has been for a reason. I was meant to be where I am right now, I guess some would call it fate, some would say it's 'written in the stars', the truth is I have no idea, but what I do know is that this is my story of loss and one which I didn't know I would be writing initially. It came without warning, nonetheless, it has given me a renewed sense of hope and determination like never before.

The potential loss of health can be a scary thought and like some of the other featured case stories, they show that often it comes without warning, so we have no time to prepare or build up our resilience. Yet, despite adversity, we somehow find a way to get through those difficult times, whether that is through good support or finding an inner strength we never knew we had.

When I spoke to my husband about writing about my experience, he was reflective and expressed his wish to write about his perspective of the journey and how he experienced his own sense of 'loss.'

12

Unexpected Health Loss (Part 2): Gareth

March 2022 is a month that will stay with me for a very long time, if not forever.

I've always considered myself a very strong person mentally who can weather any storm that comes my way, approaching any situation with strength and positivity. That month changed the way I think about the future and made me really think about 'what is round the corner'. It taught me that it is okay to allow your barriers to come down and allow yourself to feel the emotion that comes with one of life's curveballs.

I've never really had many dealings with death other than my grandparents who died at a ripe old age, although that was maybe to be expected it was still very upsetting at the time.

I've also never had any real dealings with cancer other than my grandad, so when I heard the news that my fiancé would need to attend hospital to take a further look at something that had shown up on a routine scan I would be lying if I said I wasn't scared.

During that time, I experienced a complete mix of emotions. The "man ", inside me wanted to show a strong front for Jo and give her all the love and positivity she needed, to be her shield against all the fear and negativity that could possibly happen, but I also felt so confused. What do I say if the worst should happen? What happens next? Whilst can provide all the love and positivity, I knew she would need, I had no idea or control over what was to come.

Over the week I tried to put the forthcoming appointment to the back of my mind and focus on work, my children and carrying on with "normal "life, yet, all the time, it was there, at the back of my mind. Sometimes I would allow myself to think about it and how I would somehow come to terms with a worst-case scenario, but most of the time I was putting a positive front on for Jo. Even though we had every chance of a positive outcome its human nature to fear the worst the feelings of loss were scary.

On the day of the appointment, we were sitting in the waiting room, and it suddenly became very real. By the end of that day, we were either going to be very happy and going back to living our lives and making plans for our future, or we would be making plans for a very different future altogether.

Sitting in the waiting room, I was very aware of a TV on the wall, but I couldn't tell you what was on as all I could think about was how scared Jo must have been and how I couldn't do anything to take that away. I could offer a hug, hold her hand and offer an encouraging comment, but all the time I was feeling so helpless. In that moment, I had no control, and I could not change the outcome of what was to come; that was the most frightening thing of all.

Finally, the time came for Jo to go into a scan room with the nurses, I didn't want to let her go, I wanted to go into the room and hold her hand so she would not be alone, instead

I watched her walk away into the room with the Nurse. It gave me time to reflect, I thought about what to say in either scenario and tried to put myself in Jo`s position, but nothing really made sense in my head. Her loss felt like my loss.

It seemed like an eternity but when Jo came out of that room, she had a smile on her face but still looked like she wanted to burst into tears. I heard the words I wanted to hear "It's clear".

Going through that with Jo gave me a new perspective on life, it made me realise that nothing else matters if you don't have the people you love in your life. I'm not embarrassed to say that the thought of losing Jo scared me to the point I could have cried but it definitely made us stronger as a couple.

It gave me a new outlook on our relationship in that although I already knew she was the one for me, I knew I wanted her to be my wife and live a happy and hopefully healthy life together. Don't take life for granted, as the old cliché goes, live life like every day is your last.

13

Grief and the 2020 Coronavirus (COVID-19) Pandemic

One event the world was not prepared for in 2020 was the Coronavirus (COVID-19) Pandemic, its devastation was world-wide and to this day it is still very much in the headlines. The gravity of the pandemic was felt by everyone, but more so by those who had lost loved ones whilst being forced to be apart.

Grief is a difficult emotion to process, however up to that point, the majority of people had a relative choice in being able to say their last goodbyes to their loves ones and to be there in their final moments.

The pandemic resulted in a new way of living for all of us but for those who were sick they faced being alone in isolation whether that be in a hospital, a care home or their own home. The brave carers and medical professionals who cared for our loved ones went above and beyond to try to connect us, albeit virtually, with the people we love and care about. Lines of communication were often by video calling or telephone, allowing people to feel closer, even though the virus was to keep them apart for many weeks and months. Many made extraordinary efforts to provide clients and patients with the comfort they so desperately needed, enabling them to see their families. A window into their world for many as care homes placed beds and chairs by windows so that a physical connection could be made, albeit through a pane of glass. Those treasured memories now serve to add some comfort for the friends and families who sadly found themselves bereaved due to the virus.

It is hard to even begin to put into words how grateful many people are for the dedication shown by all the frontline health workers such as the NHS, police, fire services, care homes, community care workers and the shop workers who all put others first. It was an unprecedented time which resulted in some unprecedented acts of kindness, love, and commitment.

The scale of the pandemic was incomparable to anything else and dealing with the associated loss and grief was on levels never seen before in modern times, with the number of daily deaths leaving the whole world with a sense of disbelief and shock.

As I heard the official numbers each day on television and social media, it struck me that after a while they started to become 'numbers' rather than people. That thought would often upset me as in reality, each single number was a person with a loving family, friends, work and social acquaintances, so each person's death was affecting tens if not hundreds of people. It was a very sobering thought and one which to this day still makes me feel incredibly sombre. I have many friends who lost someone in the pandemic and their grief was no less painful than pre or post pandemic loss, in fact I would consider it to be more traumatic.

The fear of this unknown disease, which was even striking down the young and healthy, it seemed relentless, however as we are all aware it was the vulnerable and the elderly who seemed to be at higher risk. We all soon realised that every single person could also potentially be at risk irrespective of gender, age, race, or socio-economic circumstances. Without warning we were all faced with a very real and sobering thought of our own mortality and how our own fragility of life was under threat. Without warning we were all faced with very real and sobering thoughts about our own mortality and the fragility of life itself.

When the World's governments announced the lock-downs, at first, I think we were all a little unsure about what they meant and how it would affect daily life, we were unprepared and not at all ready for the loss it would bring.

Truth is, there are hundreds if not thousands of stories of loss and grief associated with the pandemic, more than any book could even begin to capture.

I spoke to a lady called Denise who lost her Grandad to Covid about two months into the pandemic. I believe her story is one which echoes many other experiences.

"My Grandad was at the centre of our family, having lost my Grand-mother five years earlier, Grandad was always the beating heart of all that loved him. I remember whenever we went round, he would sit in his chair and drink his cup of tea and enjoy a slice *or two* of fruit cake, something which he said never tasted the same after Grandma died. When the pandemic hit, it was hard, suddenly our twice weekly visits had to stop and we found ourselves having to rely on phone calls instead. My Dad was still going in to take him his shopping and check up on him, but to comply with all the new rules he was the only one visiting and even then, it was only five minutes.

It was about five weeks after the beginning of the lockdown when Grandad started to feel unwell, he complained of a worsening headache and then he developed a high fever and cough. A few days later he was so unwell that an ambulance was called, and he was admitted to hospital. At that time, he was very unwell and within hours he was being transferred to intensive care as he was struggling to breathe, they explained the process they were using and that he would be given a high dose of oxygen to try to help his lungs.

The following day, the hospital called to say that he was very ill and that they needed to put him on a ventilator as his oxygen stats were critically low. Before putting him to sleep and him going on the ventilator they kindly arranged a video call so we could tell him we loved him and that we were thinking about him. Although he struggled to talk, we discussed his care as a family, and we spoke to Grandad with the help of the Nurse. He was obviously struggling to breathe, and he looked tired, he managed to talk briefly and said he would be home soon for a 'cuppa tea' and that he missed us. Whilst we all made sure we smiled for Grandad and we laughed and joked, I think we all knew the seriousness of the situation and that the likelihood of him surviving this awful virus was small, but we had to hold on to hope.

Despite going on the ventilator and the valiant efforts of the hospital staff, Grandad passed away the next day, the Consultant told us it was peaceful and that he was not in any pain, although I do remember feeling as if she was herself crying as she told us the news. I can only imagine how many of those calls she had made that day; it must have been an awful part of her daily routine. His death certificate stated Covid-19 as the reason.

After the news, I felt numb, I remember crying and feeling upset, however I also felt so angry, but I didn't know who to be directly angry with. I was angry at Covid-19 but I knew that it wasn't a person, it was an invisible disease so I had nowhere to truly direct my anger, so I struggled to process his death for quite a while.

Every day I watched the news, I saw the numbers of people dying increasing and it broke my heart to know that one of those numbers was my Grandad, but I also knew that all the other numbers meant that many people just like myself were going through the same experience, every number was a family like ours, grieving for the loss of someone they loved.

Not being able to say goodbye in person played on my mind for a long time, but I am so grateful to the hospital for allowing us to have the video call with him as at least we managed to tell him how much we loved him. He died knowing that we all loved him so very much and I hope that us being strong during that call gave him some hope and that he went to sleep knowing there was hope.

Processing all the emotions after his death was difficult, every day was different, some were okay, some were terrible. Grandad was old in years, but Covid-19 took what years he had left away and it wasn't his fault. I'm happy that he is now with Grandma but at the same time and I guess very selfishly, I wanted him to stay with us. I felt and still feel very conflicted by it all and even after three years those emotions on some days still feel just as painful.

I don't think I will ever accept how he died and I will always be angry at Covid-19 but I now want to make Grandad proud of me. I'm a Mum myself now and my beautiful son will always be told the stories about his Great-Grandad and his life. When he grows up, he will learn about the 'worlds pandemic' in his school lessons, he will learn how the pandemic changed the future of the world we live in

I find it a sobering thought that the total number of people who died to future generations will be just that 'numbers'. I'm not sure if they will ever understand the gravity of the loss, we all went through.

I will always grieve for my wonderful Grandad, but I will always be proud to say his name and to live my life happy in his memory."

Denise's story is a truly sobering account of her experience of bereavement and loss due to the pandemic and one which I'm sure will resonate with many people, not just in the UK but worldwide.

We have the statistics to provide us with the quantitative data in respect of the total deaths, however the qualitative data or narrative is much harder to quantify. Getting 'back to normal' after the pandemic to many is something that will never happen, the associated losses are insurmountable and irreversible.

The losses were not just of human life but a way of living, our jobs, livelihoods, homes and businesses were all affected. The physical and long-term impact of covid will be felt for many years, if not forever, as we count the cost of trying to live through such uncertain times.

When you add on the psychological/emotional impact, the future again looks very different indeed. Over the last few years, we have all found ways to live alongside our grief and to find a way of creating a meaningful future still, despite all the sadness.

Our united grief will always be there, but we stand together as a nation and as a world, united by our experiences. We strive to create a positive future where are losses are not forgotten but embraced to enable us to make new memories and a 'new-normal' future.

14

Back to Normal?

"Back to normal," it has so many meanings and so many different versions of itself that it's impossible to write about them all, but if I were to try to encapsulate it for the majority, I would probably say that it's finding a sense of meaning and purpose when at some point life as you knew it changed or stopped and became different. Of course, that is a very general explanation and one which may not be accurate for many. Finding that illusive meaning and purpose can be difficult; personally, I now call my life, my 'new-normal.'

After a bereavement or loss, finding a meaningful life again can be hard, there is a sense of wanting to find it but then there is also a feeling of guilt which ensues telling you that it's too early to get over the grief and that finding 'meaning' is too soon and would not be accepted by those around you. You have an overwhelming and often strong desire to go back to the life you had before and to make it all 'normal' again and to not be experiencing the pain of grief and the other difficult emotions which that entails.

Truth is, even after weeks, months and maybe even years, that yearning never really leaves you. You still crave the 'normality' of your previous life, the one before the pain and before the loss, the life which may not have been perfect but was 'your normal.'

Sadly, we cannot change the past, nor can we forget it, but we can look towards a 'new normal' and finding a new meaning to the future. Is it hard? Absolutely. Will it always be plain sailing? Absolutely not. If that were the case, we would be able to talk about grief being easy and how simple it is to just move on with no consequences.

There are so many different thought-processes after a bereavement and more questions that you ever thought possible. You feel like you can't do right for doing wrong some days and that no matter what you do it always seem to have an emotion attached to it.

It is an oscillation of emotions; one moment you may feel a sense of empowerment and optimism about the future and you start to make little steps forward and then suddenly you can feel like you have taken a huge step backwards and that it's impossible to future-proof yourself.

The journey of grief is fraught with moments like this, however over time, you do build a sense of resilience and those little moments of doubt and uncertainty become easier to navigate and adjust to.

'Moving on' from a bereavement is a term which I personally don't like, as I believe we never move on from our grief, rather it is that our life adjusts and grows around it, however this is a personal growth and is never linear.

I know personally my own grief will last forever as losing Jay was life-changing and my heart will be forever broken by his death. Although I talk about my grief regularly I still and will always have moments when I feel a little overwhelmed by it, whether that be on a specific anniversary or just in my day-to-day life. Truth is, I have learnt to accept that it's okay to not be okay sometimes and that when I have those moments of sadness, rather than dismissing them, I take a moment to reflect and remember my memories so that I acknowledge that they are very much part of my life.

My life now is full of happiness and love, but I will never forget, nor will I ever be 'over' the past, in fact I would say it makes me who I am today. I feel privileged to have been part of Jay's life and to have loved and be loved by such a truly remarkable man.

That emotive logic of wanting to take steps forward can feel incredibly heavy at times but it can also feel incredibly empowering. Taking those first steps forward is daunting, such as going back to work, starting to socialise again or even considering starting a new relationship, all of them seem a little scary at first.

Defining a meaningful life is limitless in its interpretation, but how do we even begin to define that understanding and find a way forward in all the emotional chaos? The truth is that I wish I had the answer to that conundrum, I wish I could write about the magical answer to grief and what the actual 'new normal' looks like. The truth is, we all find our own answers, in our own way and in our own time.

The one commonality we do share is that we all acknowledge that 'back to normal' is not a sentence you can use after a loss or bereavement, it is more about working towards a different new future with endless possibilities.

15

Loss of Self

Loss can be felt in so many different ways, but it is often referred to as 'losing something', as in having something physical to lose. But what if that loss was not physical, what if the loss was of a relationship, a loss of confidence, a loss of reality or a loss of faith. Loss in itself is multi-dimensional and therefore it cannot actually be isolated to one meaning or one definition.

My next case study is not one which I thought would resonate at first but as the story unfolded, I realised that it was exactly what this book represented. It shows loss from a different emotional perspective and one which represents how many people can feel at some point in their life. It reflects how our choices in life can have far-reaching consequences and how we should never make assumptions about a person's thoughts and feelings.

Janet is 49, she has two children and has been married to her husband Keith for over 25 years, having both met at university. They both have successful careers and work is important to them both, Janet works as a Specialist Nurse in a local hospital and her Husband Keith is self-employed and owns his own construction firm, they both work long and unsocial hours. They rarely spend time together but when they do, they do try to make the most of that time and go out for meals and trips away. Their marriage is strong however this was tested when their life-work balance led to an experience of 'loss' which neither of them expected.

Janet's Story

"I always wanted to be a nurse, my mum always said it was in my DNA as she was a nurse as well as my grandmother. She still tells me stories of when I was younger and used to nurse dolls with the contents of the family first aid box and how I would sit and read her text-books when they were left on the table, especially the ones with pictures and photos of often quite grisly surgeries and injuries. My mum was my hero and I revelled in telling all my friends how she helped people and how many lives she had saved; I admit probably most of those stories were embellished a little, but they made me so proud and anyone that would listen would get to hear about her life-saving heroics. My Dad was an accountant, he worked long hours, but he always made sure he was home to tuck me in bed and say goodnight, when he wasn't working, he would take me to town and buy me sweets, telling me 'Don't tell your mother'.

After school and in summer holidays, I did spend a lot of time with our Nanny Julia who was like a second mother to me. She was however quite strict and would always ensure I studied far beyond what was actually required of my usual school-work and homework. She always used to say to me that hard work is what brings success so whatever the cost you need to always be one step ahead and to always strive to be more. Little did I know at that time that her words would echo to me so poignantly throughout my career and life and play such a big part in the events which unfolded.

When my parents did get time off work, I remember summer holidays at the beach in Wales and also many trips abroad to Europe and further afield. They were wonderful holidays but I also remember them, saying that hard work reaps rewards but in to do so work must come first in order to enjoy those rewards.

My dream was to work as a Nurse just like my Mum so after achieving all A's in my school/college studies I went off to university. Leaving home was hard but as a young woman I craved independence and my own life, I loved my parents and I knew life would be different without them but I was excited to meet new people and to experience life for myself. It was made easier as I knew my parents would be okay, dad had been awarded a promotion at work and my mum had qualified as a specialist Nurse on a Neurolcgical ward so I knew their life would be kept busy by their jobs, their increasing social life and the fact they had each other.

It was while at University I met Keith, it was as they say 'love at first sight', we dated for pretty much the whole of university and when we graduated, we moved into together and were married. Keith set up his own construction business which over the first few months did really well, with his work being commended by all his customers. Word of mouth recommendations meant new business and new business meant Keith was very busy, I was incredibly proud of him, although our hours meant we didn't really see each other much.

Life was still good though, after graduating and having already started life as a Student Nurse at the local hospital I had decided what I wanted to specialise in so I was completing additional training and completing a rotation on the different wards to gain experience. I loved my job and loved working in nursing, it was worth all the hard work.

Ambition is something my parents and Julia had taught me was a good thing and that to succeed in life you had to give 110% in order to achieve your dreams, so that's the benchmark I set for myself. Outside of work, I spent my time studying or reading extra books in order to give me an advantage over my fellow colleagues. I stopped going out with friends and on more than one occasion I would realise that it was late-afternoon and I hadn't eaten anything. I was surviving on coffee and adrenaline. Keith had realised this and would often comment on needing some 'time-out' and some time away from it all, but I would always put life second and my career first.

It was during that time that I was conscious that Keith was incredibly busy with his work, he needed to work the long hours and extra days to get the contracts finished on time, as finished jobs, meant clients paying their invoices and it was those invoices which paid our mortgage. When we did manage to be in the house at the same time, he was so tired and would often fall asleep on the sofa with the TV on.

I was starting to feel a little overwhelmed at that point but I didn't want to worry Keith with my problems as he was tired himself, I was so proud of him for building up the business into the successful company it was becoming. I knew I probably did need to sit and talk to him, but it was never the right moment and it would always seem less important than everything else going on.

After a couple of years, I was starting to become physically ill and my mental health was deteriorating, but my career progression seemed worth it and at that time I was the Senior sister on the ward I worked which I enjoyed thoroughly.

It was when I was at work one day when it started to crumble. I was doing the usual ward round with the Consultant, and it came to light that an error had been made with one of the patient's files and that it was my error. There was an investigation, and it was put on my personal file; along with an official verbal warning.

Dealing with my error sat heavy on my mind and I couldn't sleep and when I did, I suffered from terrible nightmares. I did tell Keith and he was very understanding but I could tell even he was becoming weary and tired of my inability to give him any meaningful reasoning for my error, and my refusal to take some time out.

It was on a cold and wet morning in December one year when I finally found myself sitting in the staff room, sobbing, with a large pack of medication at my side, I was inconsolable and to this day I cannot remember really what led me to even think about taking them. I think deep down I wouldn't have taken them but the fact that I had even considered it was a really low point. I was sent home and was convinced that my career was over, but what actually happened was that I was referred for counselling via the hospital and I was given time off to recover.

What followed over the subsequent months was me learning to find 'me' again and whilst hard I started to see what I had lost and although it wasn't really anything materialistic, I realised that in my quest to be 'more successful' and to be the person I thought I needed to be, I lost who I actually was, which was still a Nurse, but I was also a wife, mother, friend and colleague, I think I lost sight of that along the way. All of those around me had assumed that I was coping okay when really, I wasn't. Every day, I would smile and carry on, but I now know that I was far from being okay.

I started to understand that if I had simply talked to Keith, I might have been able to prevent my break-down, but hindsight is a wonderful thing and I can't change the past but I now knew that I could change the future *(with a little continued help!).* The counsellor hasn't solved all my problems, rather she has made me think about having balance in my life and to focus on the bigger picture rather than just a narrowed version of my life.

The time off work made me realise what I had lost and although I absolutely love being a nurse, I now make time for life too. Me and Keith have recently celebrated a big wedding anniversary and instead of working, I booked leave from work, and we went away for a long weekend. I feel so happy and so content with life, even though I had to lose myself to realise it. Now, I don't make assumptions that people are okay, I make time to simply say 'how are you?' or I ask if I can help.

When you are going through a difficult time it's hard to recognise the signs but now, I have been through that, I am passionate about helping others, which includes my patients, my work colleagues, family, and friends"

16

Loss of Self

(Part 2): Keith's Story

I was brought up as an only child by my father, my mother had died when I was very young so as much as I try to remember, I think it's the photos which create the memories rather than actual memories. My father did a great job though, he was tough with me but at the same time, he always took the time to include me and it's true that I am who I am today because of him. My father worked as a builder, he did long days, but his trade meant that he was practical around the house and was always trying to fix or build something out of old materials he would find. Our weekends were spent in the garage at his workbench, building things like bird tables or fixing up old machinery.

When I left college, I decided I wanted to go to university to study Engineering and it was there that I met Janet. I remember the day we met, I saw her, and I just knew she was the girl I would spend my life with.

After we married, financially we were doing okay so I took the chance to start my own construction business. It was hard at first and although I was getting the contracts in, to be able to fulfil those contracts I had to work long hours, including most weekends, it took its toll on our relationship, especially as at the time Janet was working at the local hospital and worked shifts so even when I did finish in the evening, she would often be just leaving for work, so we were like ships in the night for a while.

In the beginning, when we did get time off work, we made the most of it and we had some wonderful holidays, which we never wanted to end, we would walk all day around local towns, drink coffee in little cafes and spend far too much money on good food, but it always reminded us of why we fell in love, and we enjoyed every precious moment together.

We certainly worked hard and we were both doing well in our jobs. After a while though I noticed Janet wasn't eating any proper meals and was starting to lose weight quite dramatically. A previous mistake had left Janet shaken initially but she seemed okay and bounced back quite well. She worked long hours so when I tried to ask if she was okay, she would tell me she was tired but was absolutely fine, I knew maybe that wasn't true and I did keep asking but I felt like I was 'nagging' so I chose to stay quiet most days, something I regret now, looking back.

I remember that day it all happened, it was December, and I was out doing some Christmas shopping when I received a call from a friend of Janet's from the hospital, she didn't really say much but said I needed to pick Janet up as she was feeling unwell. I remember thinking that she was probably just under the weather, so I made my way over to the hospital. When I walked onto the ward, I was met with a scene which I will never ever forget. Janet was sat on a chair crying, being comforted by a colleague, she looked up to me and repeatedly just kept saying sorry.

In the following days and weeks, we spoke at great length about what had happened. I felt guilty for not acting on the obvious signs and felt like I had let Janet down by not supporting her, I felt desperately sad that I had not been there for her and not being able to help her before reaching a crisis point. I knew somewhere in our busy lives we had lost each other and although we were married, shared a house, shared a bed, and shared life together, we had both forgotten what was important.

To support Janet, I immediately cut my hours at work so I could help more around the house, thankfully the business was doing well so money was not an issue, and I had a team who could pick up the work.

Recently it was our wedding anniversary, I booked a romantic weekend away and we took that time to remember why we married all those years ago. Janet started counselling and has now changed her role at the hospital so that she has more of a life-work balance.

It was a real eye opener during that time, the future could have been so different. We both lost a sense of what was important in our lives, we focused on what we thought was important instead of looking at what we had already. I wish I could turn back time, but I can't, so instead I'm going to make sure I always remember what's important in life".

Janet's story is one which many people may relate to, her external persona and personality meant that those around her were unaware of her emotional state. She was incredibly strong however, life seemed so difficult that she made choices that had consequences, they were life changing both professionally and personally.

As individuals we are inherently resilient, but at the end of the day, we are still human and just like our bodies can break if we push them too hard, our mental health can break too, but unlike bones, our mental health takes time to heal and takes a lot of support and self-belief to even start that journey of recovery.

Loss is often defined as 'losing something' but does that loss really have to be something physical? In this story, the loss was predominantly emotional, and it was clearly life-changing for both Keith and Janet. Thankfully they were both able to recognise those thoughts and feelings and they came together to reinforce and remind themselves of the bond they shared in their marriage. Their love is testament to their united strength.

17

Pet Loss

The love of a pet can be as powerful as the love for a member of the family or friend, in some cases it can be more! Some would even argue that a pet isn't just a pet, they are indeed an integral much-loved part of the family with their presence bringing both love and companionship to millions of people across the world.

Pet owners spend all their pet's life caring and nurturing for them, ensuring that they are given the best life possible. The daily life of an average pet owner often revolves around scheduling work and life commitments around them to ensure their care needs are met, often to the detriment of themselves. Owning a pet is a huge responsibility, and comes with a great accountability for their health and welfare, however the rewards far outweigh those responsibilities in the love that is returned.

When a pet dies it can be life-changing for many people and it can feel just as traumatic as a human bereavement. The feelings of loss are just as powerful and the associated grief just as painful.

In my next story Sally describes her journey when her dog Barney was diagnosed with cancer. Despite all the best efforts by her Vet, he sadly passed away a few months later. The story captures the special bond between Sally and Barney and the overwhelming grief she experienced after he died.

"It was the summer of 2014 when we decided to get our first dog, it was a big decision as we both worked full-time, but we had come up with a plan so we could both be at home regularly throughout the day. We had saved up some money and when the time was right, we set about our search for a rescue dog. A couple of weeks later, we went to a local rescue centre and within five minutes we had found our 'Barney'. He was a small terrier who was just over a year old, he was very timid but was perfect in every way. After completing all the checks and paperwork, a few days later we were on our way home, with Barney sitting on the back seat in his brand-new harness.

The following weeks were a learning process for all of us, like meeting a new friend, we had to get to know each other and learn our little quirky mannerisms, but we did, and after a year, I was fluent in doggie barks and whines. Barney was a very loving dog and very intuitive to any changes in the house. When I was having a bad day, he always knew how to snuggle up to me and give me his big brown eyes, he had a way of always making a bad day better. He loved long walks and being outside but was equally happy lying on his favourite blanket by the open fire.

It was when Barney was just over six years old that we noticed a small lump on his leg, it wasn't very big and didn't seem to bother him, but after a week, we decided to get it checked by the vet. The news from the vet that afternoon, changed everything. The lump was malignant and whilst they did not think it had spread, they recommended an amputation to save his life. A week later he was at the vets having the life-saving surgery.

As the days and weeks went by Barney recovered incredibly well, it was remarkable to see him running again like nothing had changed, he was our miracle dog.

A year after his after his surgery, Barney was suddenly taken ill, we rushed him to the vets and were told that Barney was very sick and that it looked as if the cancer was back and had spread and that there was nothing, they could do to help him. We were advised that due to his suffering it would be kinder to let him go as his pain would only increase, and the outcome was ultimately the same.

We took Barney home and that night we stayed by his side, we talked to him, kept him warm and never left him. The vet had given him pain killers so he was in no pain and seemed comfortable. The following morning, we made the trip back to the vets and said goodbye to our Barney for the last time. It was the hardest journey I have ever had to make.

In the days after Barney died, I was just numb, I remember crying all the time, I felt a pain in my stomach like I had never felt before, and my heart felt like it was breaking. The house was quiet and the chair he used to always sit on was empty, I felt a loneliness which I can't put into words. Barney was just a dog to many, but to me he was my best friend, he was always there to comfort me when I was sad, and was always there to make me smile with his crazy play-times.

After a few weeks, my mood was very low, I dreaded returning from work to an empty house, and I was struggling with anything which needed even a small amount of concentration. People would try to offer advice and would be sympathetic but comments like "well he's in a better place" and "you can get another dog like Barney" really didn't help. Although I do think they were from a place of trying to be nice, they felt emotionless and uncaring.

We didn't have children of our own, so Barney was my child, albeit in canine form, the loss just felt massive, every time I went out, I would see a dog like him, when I watched tv, there would be dogs on there, I just missed him so much.

It was at that time that I contacted someone who specialised in supporting people with pet bereavement, for the first time there was someone who understood. During that time, I slowly started to come to terms with my grief and find ways of coping with the loss so that I could start to feel better. It didn't happen overnight, but I did find a way through it, by talking to the amazing counsellor and finding helpful ways to deal with the loss.

I still have days when I miss Barney and when I see a dog like him in the street, I find myself thinking about him, but I now smile and I try to remember all of the funny and memorable moments we shared.

Barney wasn't just a dog, he was my family and my best friend, he was the person who listened to me moan about my day, but also the dog that jumped up all excited at the thought of a treat or a walk. The grief I felt was no less than that of a family or friend grief, it was very real and incredibly painful.

When I speak to people now and they say to me about getting back to normal, I just cannot understand what they mean, I find it impossible to forget Barney. Normal was when Barney was sat on my lap and when he barked at the birds in the park. Nowadays, I like to share my memories rather than being so overwhelmed by them. I try to remember those happy memories and although I do have some sad moments, I have found ways with the support to find a way through them.

At the time of writing this I am very happy to say that I do now have another bundle of fur, a beautiful rescue terrier called Lola, who although in her older years of life, still has so much love to give and has brought me a sense of belonging again.

Even though the grief of losing Barney was and is still painful to think about, I am so grateful to have been part of his life and to be the one who loved him"

Sally's story echoes the experience of many people and is an area of grief which is not sometimes given the publicity it rightly deserves. A relationship with a pet is unique, the pain of grief can be just as traumatic and painful as human bereavement, maybe more so.

With pets we must rely on our instincts and our awareness of their body language to understand their thoughts and physical ailments. Over time we get to know our pets intuitively and learn all their quirky and familiar behaviours. It is that established bond, which is based on mutual trust and love that allows us to care for our pets as we would a member of the family.

18

Loss of Control

Have you ever felt like you were not good enough, like everything you do never seems to be sufficient? Despite giving your utmost to be or do what is right or what is expected, it never quite goes to plan! Does this sound familiar or do you think it is maybe a pessimistic way to look at a situation you're in?

Truth is, irrespective of how you see the situation we can all doubt ourselves sometimes and we can occasionally view life from a 'cup half empty' perspective rather than the positive 'cup half full' thought process.

The main thing to remember with the 'half-empty' days is that there will always be 'half-full' days too, but I'd be lying if that was an easy thing to say and do when you are having a shockingly bad day and it is you versus the world!

There is a quote I once heard which I now use quite often in my counselling work, as I find it quite poignant and valuable.

"Some days you get up, nothing goes right and you have the most awful day which just keeps getting worse, you feel physically and emotionally drained. Always remember that the day will end and the following morning you can reflect on the day before and say that you 'got through it'. Think about that day and remember that to date, your track record of getting through each day has been 100%'. Despite at the time feeling as if you wouldn't get through it, you did, and you will again. We are all stronger than we think, even when we doubt ourselves"

Despite some of the darkest days, we somehow get through the day, on those days it takes a level of inner strength that most people don't even know that they have.

Personally, I have had more days like this than I can even begin to remember, there have been so many days that I have felt so desperately overwhelmed or sad that my heart would just hurt and feel beyond repair. I am sure that there will be more of those types of days in the future, I only hope they are few and far between. However, like the quote, I remind myself "my track record of getting through each day is 100%".

We all have bad days, however there are days where you feel completely overwhelmed and those days are the ones which stick in our memories the most.

My next story is a lady called Belinda. She shared her story with me about how she felt when her son was suddenly faced with a potential medical diagnosis. The reason I thought it was relevant was that her story was the loss of control over her son's potential health diagnosis. At the time, getting through each day was hard and it took a level of strength that even Belinda didn't know she had.

In the summer of 2021, Belinda was faced with every parent's nightmare, when her seventeen-year-old son discovered a lump in his neck. He had seen his GP and had been referred to the local hospital for investigations. This is her story in her words.

"As a parent I've spent every single day since my children were born thinking how I can keep them safe. Whilst you cannot wrap children in cotton wool, you always want to keep them away from harm, both physically and emotionally. Whether it be protecting them from falling off their first bike or being a shoulder to cry on after their first relationship break-up, it is a natural feeling to want to shield them.

One thing you can't protect your children from (within reason!) is illness, whether it be a common cold or something more serious. As much as we try, sometimes they do get ill, and all we can do is trust the medics around us to provide the care and medication they need to recover.

Throughout the years, the children have given me more than a few sleepless nights with various illnesses and injuries. From broken bones to respiratory illnesses, I seem to have visited hospitals on more than a few occasions needing anything from a simple anti-biotic to surgeries to fix bones! Each time, irrespective of their seriousness, the feelings are the same, you worry and the anxiety of not knowing what's happening never gets any easier.

When my son found a lump on the side of his throat, those feelings awoke like a vicious storm of emotion in my heart. Whilst on the exterior I was calm and I was reassuring, inside I must admit to feeling incredibly anxious and worried. Three years earlier I had sat in a hospital room listening to a doctor explain to us about my own father's diagnosis of terminal Pancreatic Cancer after having symptoms for only one month. Whilst I knew in my mind that the chances were maybe slim of my son having such a bad diagnosis, the feelings were still very real, and it stirred a level of anxiety in me that was instantly recognisable. I maintained a calm and reassuring composure for his sake and I continued with life as we knew it, trying to block out the thoughts of any negative thinking. I think the truth is that if I really sat and thought about the possibility that it could be cancer then I would not be able to carry on. I could not begin to think about how I could possibly hear the news that my own son was ill, it was inconceivable and unthinkable.

The day before his appointment, the only thing I could do was keep busy as thinking about what the following day held was too overwhelming and just ended up in me getting upset. I actually cannot remember much of the day, I was busy, yet I could not tell you what I did!

On the morning of the appointment, after a night of broken sleep, I lay in bed thinking about how the day would unfold and if we would be looking forward to celebrating his birthday which was the following month, or if we would be preparing for an unimaginable scenario. After getting ready we set out to the appointment.

We chatted in the car, but the atmosphere was one of pure anxiety and trepidation, but he was surprisingly upbeat. In that moment though in my eyes he wasn't an adult, he was that little 7lb baby in my arms, who just needed to be nurtured and cared for and told that nothing in the world mattered apart from him feeling safe.

Walking through the hospital I was again taken back to when I walked through with my father. I remember walking quite fast but at the same time it was like time was standing still, or maybe I just wanted it to stand still so I didn't have to go through the next few minutes/hours. My heart was beating so fast that I felt light-headed, my hands felt cold, and I couldn't decide if I needed to sit down or walk around to keep myself busy.

As I looked at my son, I was again reminded of sitting in the hospital myself a few years back when I was having checks for my own cancer scare, it all felt too much to deal with.

As we sat waiting, on the outside I was the Mum he needed, I was strong and there to deal with anything that happened, even though on the inside my heart was crying.

As he was called through, we were shown to another waiting area, my heart sank as I realised it was the same waiting area I sat with my father when he was there. I sat down and acted as if everything was okay until we were called through to the consultant and again, it was the same examination room. I hesitated as I sat down on the familiar chair, knowing that the last time I had been in there was when dad was still alive and was very much hopeful, thinking that it was all 'a bunch of nonsense and that the docs would fix him up if he was ill'.

I sat there listening to the exchange of conversation between the consultant and my son until we were told that it was nothing to worry about. I am a woman of many words, but it is hard to explain how I felt in that moment. I kept the strong exterior, inside I wanted to either fall to the floor or give him the biggest hug. Instead, I smiled and we walked out together, composed and reassured.

That feeling that I may lose something so precious to me was a scary moment and one which I will never forget, it made me truly appreciate how much love I have inside of me for my children. Every now and then they do things that make me cringe but losing them is something I never want to experience ever again.

I always hold my son that little bit tighter nowadays and I always tell him I love him. I know I can't protect him completely from everything bad in this world, but I will always be there when he needs me, the thought of losing him is something I just cannot put into words."

Although it was a happy outcome in this story, it made me think of those parents who maybe come out of these types of appointments having received bad news instead of good. Sadly, I have a couple of friends who have lost a child and I find it incredibly difficult to even comprehend the level of sadness they have been through, but I am also in awe of their tenacity, strength and resilience to be able to share their experiences and talk so openly about their memories.

If I am honest, I really don't think I have even a small notion of what it must have been like, so in an enlightening kind of way this story has taught me a very valuable and sobering lesson and one which I will never ever forget.

Belinda's story has allowed me to reflect on my work as a Grief Specialist. I have always believed that I will never perfectly understand what someone is going through after a loss or bereavement, but I can relate to the associated feelings and emotions having been through that experience myself. However, for anyone reading this who has lost a child or is currently going through an illness with their child/children, I absolutely share my respect and admiration. You have the strength of a thousand people inside you, and your courage is astounding.

This is particularly relevant to my next story from a lady called Danielle, whose struggles with pregnancy and miscarriage has been life-changing in so many ways.

19

Miscarriage and Parenthood

Trying for a baby can be one of the most wonderful times in a person's life with the excitement of bringing another life into the world and creating a family bringing so much joy and love. However, it doesn't always go to plan and there are many women who struggle to concieve, for a number of reasons, the emotions of this being incredibly overwhelming and often life-changing.

If a pregnancy is successful, sadly there can be further complications which mean that the pregnancy does not go to term. Miscarriage is one of the most common kinds of pregnancy loss, affecting around one in four pregnancies, with most being sudden and unexpected.

Experiencing problems with fertility and/or miscarriage is devastating for all those affected with the feelings of pain and loss lasting many months and sometimes years. Many women may feel like its their fault or that they did something wrong and this can feel quite overwhelming in the early weeks and months after the loss.

Equally, it is also important to note that although physically it is a woman who experiences the miscarriage, it also affects partners too. The loss can be just as painful and distressing for the partner as it is for the woman. Those who experience a miscarriage may find that they feel incredibly lonely as they not only come to terms with the immediate physical feelings of loss but the loss of the hope they had for the pregnancy/birth.

In time, the feelings may become less painful, however the reminder on anniversaries can be a difficult time to navigate as you have both the date of the loss and the expected birth date, with both being emotionally significant.

My next story is incredibly powerful and, in many ways, upsetting. It is written by a very brave lady called Danielle who shared her story about her struggle in getting pregnant and her experience and anguish from a number of miscarriages.

Reader caution: Danielle's words are her own and at times she describes some upsetting scenes so if you have been through this type of loss, please be aware that this story is quite upsetting to read at times.

"I lost my first baby in September 2017, my second in December 2017 and my third in March 2021.

I don't know where to start in writing my story, it's such a long one and seems to be circular at times. I always wanted to be a mother; I've never been so sure of anything else in my entire life. From the age of 4 if anyone ever asked me what I wanted to be when I was older, my answer was always that I wanted to be a mum (not counting the time I wanted to be a doctor or Astronaut).

Between the ages of 14 and 20 I was with the love of my life but when he said he never wanted to have children, I left him, the ironic thing is that he is now a dad. In a sense I am already a 'mother' albeit to the other children in my life, but the reality is that I do not have my own children in a physical sense. I don't have little people running around my house, I don't have birthdays or Christmas's to get excited for, or piles of little clothes in my kitchen needing to be washed, I have nothing to show for my journey.

I keep thinking where do I begin with my story? Do I start at the age of 11 where sex education and my upbringing always led you to believe that having children was something you did in later life once a career was established, and you were financially comfortable enough? My early career as a biology teacher and PSHE lead always denoted that you should teach about the importance of contraception etc, and rightly so, however, no one ever discussed the fact that in some cases having children is not a given and that in fact it can be an incredibly difficult dream to achieve. During schooling people are so often warned about the chances of unwanted or early pregnancy, but no one ever discusses the darker side, the side when you cannot carry a child or have the family you always 'assumed' would be yours when the time is right.

I met my husband at the age of 22, we were best friends during our teacher training, a few years later, after we had both experienced poor relationships, we became a couple. We lived together for a few years before getting married. A year prior we decided I would come off the pill for my body to adjust so that once we were married, we could actively begin trying for a family of our own. We had the dream, the most amazing 'fairy-tale' wedding and upon arriving home from our dream honeymoon we found that we were expecting a baby. I remember at the time thinking how incredibly blessed we were and how lucky we were to have everything just 'fall into place.' Alas, shortly after our wonderful news I began to 'spot', I went to the Dr who reassured me that she too bled a lot during her early pregnancy and put me on bed rest for a week. However, it was not meant to be, and we lost our baby a few days later.

A few months later, I suspected I was pregnant again, I kept my suspicions to myself for a week or two; too scared to share with anyone through fear of the same thing happening again. I did a pregnancy test on my husband's birthday which confirmed that we were indeed expecting another baby. I had quite bad morning sickness with this pregnancy and felt like I was googling every symptom every second of the day to check if things were 'normal' or a sign that something might be wrong. It was a mix of emotions during those weeks, feelings of being so blessed to have been able to conceive again mixed with feelings of guilt for conceiving so quickly and anxiety as to how this pregnancy would progress. I was in a turmoil of emotions, terrified of the same thing happening, feeling emotionally and physically too weak to be able to comprehend how I would cope if things didn't turn out for the best.

I was constantly telling myself that our first experience of pregnancy was 'bad luck' and didn't mean that this one would end in the same way. I will never forget the day that our worst fears were confirmed. I was teaching that Tuesday afternoon and my class were partaking in a dance workshop. I went to the toilet afterwards and my worst fears came true, blood. I went to my head of department who was also a good friend of mine and burst into tears. She drove me home and once I got there; I didn't know what to do. Do I climb into bed and hide and pretend it isn't happening? Do I seek medical help in the hope that they can wave some sort of 'magic wand' and make it all ok?

As I walked into my GP, it was closing time and the lady on reception was so lovely. She called the hospital straight away and got me a scan appointment for the following day. My sister, who lived with us at the time, drove me there after a night of sobbing my heart out and fitful sleep. She almost had to carry me into the department, I was numb with grief, terrified of what may or may not be about to be confirmed. I lay down for my scan and stared at the right angles on the panels in the ceiling, trying to focus on anything other than what I may be about to be told.

That was one of the longest few minutes of my life, I didn't have to ask, I knew what the silence and the constant moving of the scanning implement meant. They called my sister through who helped to dress me and asked me to wait in the room with her, we held hands and stared out of the window together, I couldn't form the words, I couldn't form tears, I was numb. My sister called my work to inform them and took me home, I wanted to cry, I wanted to scream, I wanted to smash everything I owned, so it was a surprise to myself and her that instead I decided to redecorate the kitchen. My husband came home that evening and found me standing on the work surface painting above the sink, it was then emotion hit and once the tears came, it felt like they would never stop.

No one talks about the physical pain of losing a pregnancy, I spent the next few days in agony, eventually passing a large clot. I screamed and my sister came into the bathroom, unsure of what to make of it myself, was I holding what remained of my pregnancy in my hands? Neither of us knew what to do, what can you do? We wrapped the clot in the tissue and flushed the toilet, it seemed so cruel, so heartless. The clot seemed to signify the reality of what had been lost, whether physically significant or not, and to flush it away seemed barbaric. I hid in my bed and did not emerge for many days.

The weeks following were hard on us, so many 'what-if's', so much guilt of blaming myself, had I done something wrong? Had I not been eating right? What if I hadn't participated in my classes dance workshop that afternoon. The rational mind and words of others would say absolutely not, it's one of those things. The mind of a mother who has failed her two pregnancies and her husband in the space of a few months does not.

I threw myself into Christmas that year, trying to distract myself from everything although constantly reminding myself I should be celebrating with our 'bump' and berating myself for the losses we had endured the preceding months. My husband and I went on a short break between Christmas and New Year to try and take our mind off things and we spent some much-needed quality time together. The emotions of the past few months had been too much and had taken a toll on our relationship. During that trip I received a call from my GP surgery to say that they would not put my repeat prescription through that I had ordered a week before for my antidepressants because of my pregnancy. I stood still and then had to explain that the pregnancy had been unsuccessful, they then apologised as they had not read my notes properly.

The following day I had a social media message from someone I knew asking me about the plans for a friend's baby shower the following month. Her pregnancy had been announced shortly before my wedding and she was due to give birth in a couple of months. That, as well as the call from the surgery the previous day threw my world into a spin again. I couldn't comprehend at that point finishing planning a baby shower when I had so recently lost my own babies.

Instead of explaining how overwhelmed and raw I still felt I threw myself into finishing the planning of the baby shower. It was a lovely day, however, at the back of my mind I could not stop thinking about the babies I had recently lost and of the celebrations I would never experience. I felt so guilty for those thoughts and feelings, like the worst person in the world. I couldn't hold it together any longer and feigned a headache and a trip to the shop to get some paracetamol. I drove to the nearest car park and sobbed my heart out until there were no more tears to come. I 'pulled myself together' and returned, all smiles and ready to help with the clearing away. I have no idea how I made the 45-minute car journey home through the tears of sadness, frustration, and guilt.

When her baby was born, I will never forget holding her for the first time, she was the most beautiful, precious thing, it was then I truly realised what a gift having a child is, a true blessing.

Over the next 18 months my husband and I tried to conceive again, to no avail. At one point we were away travelling, and I was feeling particularly tired and nauseous, we talked about doing a test but deep down neither of us could face the outcome whichever that may be whilst away from our family and friends for so long. On reflection I do not regret that decision not to test, I don't think either of us could have coped with the confirmation of another loss at that point.

We decided at that point to seek medical advice and were referred to a clinic. After lots of tests and discussions the conclusion was that we should try Clomid or go straight to IVF to make our dream a reality. We went away and had lots of conversations, some of which were very difficult. We both had friends who had been through IVF and knew the emotional and physical toll it could take on couples. We decided to keep trying naturally for another six months before going back to the clinic to make our decision if we had not been successful in that time.

During that time, we had also applied to be respite foster carers. Our initial applications had been successful, and we were going to regular 'classes' and having home visits before going to panel in a few months' time. The process for this can feel quite invasive and without realising it was increasingly putting our marriage under strain. We managed to get through Christmas that year, however, a few weeks later I moved out of our marital home and our marriage never recovered. We still remain friends and are both now in new relationships. Do I think our marriage would have ended had we managed a successful pregnancy? The honest answer is no, I do not. I could write a separate chapter on the loss of my marriage and the beautiful home we built together, so that's all I will say about that.

I entered a new relationship and quite unexpectedly a year in we found out that we were pregnant. I'd had quite an irregular cycle during that time, so it was difficult to know how far along we were with the pregnancy at that point. I have to say it took us a while to process the news, we were both incredibly shocked given my history and the advice of the doctors. I approached this pregnancy with less apprehension than my second. I think because so much time had passed and that I was with a new partner, my brain kept telling me that this was fate, it was meant to be, miracles do happen. I reassured myself by reading stories of other couples who had had surprise successful pregnancies after many years of trying. Despite this, deep down I was absolutely terrified. I had a stressful job at this point with even more pressure due to the constantly changing Covid restrictions, I was tired, drained, and unwell most days.

One Friday I began to get sharp pains in my lower abdomen, the panic swept through me, the adrenaline making me vomit, 'please no, please God I will do anything to save this pregnancy' I told myself over and over again. An hour later work decided to let me go home where I went on bed rest. We were in limbo the whole weekend, not knowing what to do, not knowing if, when and how to access help. I lay in bed, dreading going to the toilet each time as the spotting got heavier and heavier. On the Monday my partner managed to get through to a midwife who reassured him spotting was normal and not to panic and that they would see how I was in a few days and if the situation was the same then they would make an appointment (bear in mind we were on lock down restrictions at this time, so it was difficult to see medical professionals). I didn't know what to do, I couldn't just lie there not knowing what was happening, was I still a mother? Had we lost our baby?

I booked a private scan at a local clinic, I drove there in tears, not wanting to go in, not wanting confirmation of what I felt in my gut had already happened but at the same time being unable to continue not knowing.

I lay on the bed and picked a spot on the ceiling, it was almost a replay of what I had gone through three years previously, lying on the bed whilst the sonographer was searching, trying every angle and pressure to try and find that tiny heartbeat. I looked at her face and just nodded, we both knew there was no saving this pregnancy. I drove home and fell apart; how could this be happening? How could life be so cruel? We were good, loving people, we didn't have much in terms of money, but we had a loving home ready for our child.

The next few days went by in a blur, the emotional grief was intolerable, however so was the physical. The next few months were incredibly hard for us both, with increasing work pressures and trying to grieve but not knowing how. How do you grieve a child you've never met or never held? There are no memories or photographs to reflect on, only made-up memories that you create in your head, birthdays, trips to the seaside that never happened and never will happen. We went through phases between being so close with each other to being distant. At one point I just couldn't cope any longer and I took an overdose with the intent to take my own life, that was the lowest point of my life.

The next six months were incredibly difficult for us both, I began to recover day by day, each day just getting out of bed felt like a mountain to climb. My partner was incredibly patient with me during those dark days, and I honestly don't think I would be sitting here writing this account if it wasn't for him. I quit my stressful job and literally started from scratch. I rebuilt myself, my relationship, and my life. I even went back on the contraceptive pill, which may sound counter-productive when you are trying to start a family but I needed to protect myself and my partner while we could heal as much as you can following loss. There are days still when the grief envelopes you and feel you are walking on treacle.

Anniversaries of due dates are particularly hard, you imagine what you should have been doing, and it can be easy to get lost in those thoughts but ultimately, they are not going to do any good. Those memories will never be made, those babies have passed to heaven and it is important to accept that and look to the future. My experience of loss has changed me forever, and the silver lining I would like to take from our experiences as I continue to rebuild my life is that I can use my experiences to help other people going through miscarriage or infertility, and for that I am incredibly grateful.

During my journey I felt a rainbow of emotions, initially I felt deep sadness, anger, and frustration at what was happening. I then turned my emotions to myself, I was incredibly cruel to myself during that time, I felt like a failure, not worthy, a terrible partner and terrible mother.

Over time those feelings meandered, I began to feel jealousy towards those who were more fortunate with their fertility, I had feelings of guilt, towards my partner for having to support me and to my family for taking away their chance to be an aunty/grandparent, and for letting other people's dreams down too.

I also over time, under the umbrella of negative emotions, felt privileged, blessed to have been able to carry a pregnancy, to experience pregnancy, even for such a short time, a privilege some couples do not get to experience. I also feel that as I became stronger, I feel able to use my experience to help others, to listen with understanding, to share my story so that others do not necessarily feel alone in their experience, or the feelings they are feeling.

There have been many setbacks, starting with the loss of my marriage. My lowest point was the point at which I tried to take my own life, the guilt I felt towards my partner and family, for putting them through the stress. The journey is ongoing, it will never end, you feel that you are getting back into the swing of 'normality' and you see yet another friend posting about their pregnancy on Facebook, and you feel like you have been punched in the stomach. Instantly those emotions come flooding back, anger, guilt, jealousy. I feel ashamed to admit it but jealousy is an overriding emotion in this journey and I feel incredibly guilty for it but I cannot help it, I am a human being. I can mask my emotions but I cannot ultimately control them.

Throughout my journey, what I have found hard is the reactions of other people. Through no fault of their own, people try to be reassuring and say things like 'these things happen', 'you can always try again', 'it's maybe for the best, something was probably wrong'. I can honestly say that at no point have those phrases made me feel better in anyway. In fact, quite the opposite, they fill me with anger and frustration, even to this day. I have also since found that it has been difficult to maintain relationships with friends who have been blessed with children. Not through any outward jealousy, but because their lives become recentred around their children and their family and that as someone who does not share in that themselves it can be difficult to maintain connections and things in common. From a personal point of view, it can be difficult, especially when hiding feelings of jealousy or sadness when they are moaning about things their children have or haven't done, it is exhausting. It is easier to avoid the situation than try to battle the flood of emotions that inevitably come.

I accessed very little support when going through my journey. I pushed my feelings away; I pushed those I love away to try and protect myself. It took an incredibly long time for me to acknowledge and share my feelings. I feel like this contributed to my very low point of suicide and I wish I had reached out for help and support sooner. I wish I had known then that there is absolutely no shame in the emotions I was feeling and that actually when you speak to people with similar experiences that they too have gone through similar feelings, it helps. Each person's journey is their own and there is no right or wrong way to feel or deal with things. I am now (at the time of writing this) waiting for bereavement counselling which I hope will help to deal with the emotions as I continue my journey. My thoughts and feelings will never go away, nor do I wish them to, my journey is a part of me and who I have become, however, I do feel that by speaking about them may help me to deal with them in a healthier manner.

I found that people were either incredibly supportive (sometimes to the point of feeling smothered) or they shied away from the situation. Sometimes it was easier when people stayed away because it allowed me to shut down, avoid people and avoid acknowledging my feelings.

In a very positive way though, this journey has cemented what was already an incredible bond with my sister. Her response has always been very patient, but she is always very frank in her thoughts, and I have always appreciated and respected her for that. I never express my feelings or emotions to anyone other than her, I wear a well-practised mask. She encouraged me to write down my feelings during those moments and they have helped me to find a sense of calm and to feel less angry and less jealousy towards others.

One of the most positive elements of this journey has been that I don't take anything for granted, ever. Before this experience I assumed I'd get married, have a good job, have a lovely family, and go on holiday once a year. This experience turned all those things upside down and made me realise that we create the life we want, it is not something that is handed on a plate to us, nor is it something we should ever assume. I wake up every day and I thank God I am still alive and able to do so. When I wanted to take my life, I was incredibly unwell, my mind was poorly, and I am so grateful to have survived and recovered from that. I make the most of each day and opportunity God brings, I rarely say no these days. I don't want to live my life just for myself but for the people who didn't get a second chance to rebuild their lives and for my unborn children, to make them proud and to make my family and partner proud.

Day to day I have two frames of mind, one is where I feel emotionally vulnerable on the edge of tears and one is where I feel blessed and lucky to be alive, not wanting to waste a moment. From the outside no one would ever know which of these two mindsets I am in but inside I do. When people say things like 'things will go back to normal' the mindset I am in at the time really does define how it makes me feel. For example, vulnerable me wants to cry and feel sad and grieve that 'normal' that will never be again, blessed me, who was given a second chance at life sees it as an opportunity to build the 'new normal' the normal I want for my life.

As far as I am concerned there is no going back to 'normal' the losses I have experienced over the past six years mean that there is no 'back to normal,' too much has changed and too much has been lost for that to ever happen. There is however, the new normal. My losses are a part of me and who I am now, they have shaped the person I have become and although there is a lot of negativities involved in my story those events have also created a more patient, accepting person through those hardships. I am excited in a way to create my 'new normal' yet at the same time apprehensive, what do I want that normal to look like? What if I don't get it right a second time? I have learnt recently to take each day as a unit on its own, as looking too far ahead and questioning the 'what if's' is not helpful and creates unnecessary anxieties.

I can honestly say I have no idea what my future looks like. If you had told me six years ago when I was walking up the aisle where I would be today, I would have laughed, maybe cried, but not believed a word of it. If I think about the future too much, I get frustrated by the things I have lost and sometimes anxious about the future I want to create and making the 'right' decisions. I look at each day as a fresh opportunity to be the best version of me, to help people, and to carve a bright future. If I make good decisions every day then this will build a brighter future and continue to shape me into the person I want to be, I find this much easier to approach than looking at the vast journey ahead and the potential pitfalls which I may encroach along the way.

When I look at where I am from our first loss, I am a completely different individual. I am more in tune with recognising and understanding my own emotions and although those emotions can be difficult to deal with at times, I am ten times stronger, and I hope to use this strength to help others who may be experiencing a similar journey to my own.

Looking forward I am never sure whether doing something to commemorate these anniversaries could potentially cause more harm than good. I generally approach them with mixed emotions, sadness at the loss but also with hope for the future. With my sister's encouragement I have learnt to allow myself to feel whatever I feel at these times and to not feel guilty for whatever those emotions may be.

If I were in a room now with a person going through the same situation as mine, I would say don't be tempted to hide away and enclose yourself. It is so easy to shut people out and to try and shut your emotions out and that is ok for a little while, however, the longer you shut yourself away the harder it is to reach out and ask for support. Try to allow yourself to feel whatever you need to feel. Be patient with yourself and be kind, it can be a journey of huge ups and huge downs and you have got the strength to get through this, take small steps on your journey, don't worry about where the map is leading, worry about where you are stood right now"

Listening to Danielle's story and hearing her speak so honestly and candidly about her experience, it felt quite over-whelming to hear about the loss and grief she has experienced and yet her courage and tenacity is phenomenal. She spoke from the heart which I know will resonate with so many people, in so many ways.

Danielle's story is powerful and yet beautifully truthful about how even though the grief can be overwhelming, in time it is possible to use that grief as a recovery tool and to find your own unique meaning to the future. Her experience will never leave her, it is part of who she is but her life is still full of love, hope and a determination to be happy.

Danielle is truly inspirational and I feel privileged that she chose to share her story and to highlight such a personal story of loss and grief. Her bravery in sharing her journey I know will offer an incredible amount of support to others who may have been/or are going through a similar situation.

20

Triggers and Grief

Anyone who is going through or has been through a bereavement will know that 'triggers can come out of nowhere and without notice. Within seconds, you can be transported back to that first day once again! You can be having a really good day and then, bang, your body is shaking, and your brain is like fog again, sound familiar?

What many books don't tell you is that those triggers happen more often than you think. They could just be little moments of reflection and you may be able to carry on with your day after gathering your feelings and thoughts, or they can be absolute humdingers that stop you in your tracks and throw you off balance for hours, days or weeks.

Even after a few years, you can still have moments like this regularly, sometimes they pass relatively quickly, but more often than not, they just happen unexpectedly. In those moments it is often best to firstly, acknowledge them and then take the time to process the attached emotions. It is often helpful to have some self-help techniques on hand for times like these. It could be that you go for a walk, or you listen to your favourite music or even take a hot shower or bath. There really is no wrong answer to how you develop your own techniques for dealing with triggers, it is just what works for you.

To list all the potential triggers would be bordering on impossible as I'm pretty sure the list would just keep growing, especially if we really sat and thought about it.

Personally, my most random trigger is seeing a Tractor. Jay was infatuated by tractors and we often made fun of his quirky fascination with all things 'farming.' although this originated from his childhood as his family worked in the agricultural profession so from an early age he was immersed in the 'farming lifestyle.'

He was proud of his knowledge and even had an interactive farming game set-up on his computer, much to our amusement when we would walk past the room to hear cow's 'mooing' and chickens 'clucking', to which he would reply that he's just bringing the 'cows in for the night'. I never did understand the appeal, but it was just his thing and was one of his more amusing qualities, which still makes me smile today.

A common and poignant trigger for the majority of the bereaved is Christmas time. Christmas for many is a joyous time, but for those who are bereaved it can be a time to reflect and remember the friends and family who are no longer with us. Grief does not disappear over the festive season; in fact, some would say it is heightened as we remember and grieve for our memories of past Christmas's with our loved ones.

It is true, after a bereavement, Christmas is different, both physically and emotionally, it is hard and it can be difficult and, in the lead, up to Christmas, the feelings of sadness can feel overwhelming at times.

Reflecting on my own grief, I find it comforting to remember the special memories of loved ones, in particular my Grandad. He loved Christmas and with his unique sense of humour, he was always a shining light over the festive season. His ability to always eat a huge Christmas dinner, as well as two desserts was always a source of great amusement on Christmas Day. Those are the memories which feel so special and meaningful. At first, after a bereavement memories like these can feel painful and upsetting, however over time they become treasured mementos in time.

My fondest memories of Jay are that he would always go above and beyond to get the funniest Christmas jumper and would always be the one in the turkey hat around the Christmas table, making us all laugh. He was a genuinely funny man who was never one to back out of a challenge or an opportunity to be the joker.

I remember, the first Christmas after Jay died. We were in the shops doing some Christmas shopping and we noticed a funny Christmas jumper. My instant thought was 'Jay would love that'. I stopped walking and stood looking at the jumper, questioning why my mind had instantly jumped to the thought of Jay wearing it and laughing. It may seem like such a small moment in time, but those are the triggers which can be difficult at first. It is like a constant reminder of your loss, which can be emotionally significant in those few weeks and months. In time, those moments don't disappear at all, they simply get less overwhelming.

Nowadays at Christmas, we laugh, and we share good food and drink; my sons wear the infamous turkey hat as we pull crackers to celebrate the day.

After a bereavement or loss special occasions can still be special, and they can still be full of laughter, love, and special memories. Many people like to mark a special occasion in a subtle way, for instance lighting a candle or placing a photo in a prominent place. However, you choose to mark the special occasion, it doesn't matter how small or big the memory is, it just has to be right for you.

It is incredibly important to be aware that it is okay to feel sad sometimes, after all our love and memories will never lessen, they will always be part of who we are. The love we had and still have, is what gives us hope and the capability to keep going and to remember those who are no longer sat beside us with the greatest of warmth and adoration.

With triggers being a significant part of the bereavement and loss journey, memories can be at the forefront of your mind and it can be difficult to ignore them, but then again, why would you want to ignore them? Essentially those memories are happy recollections which brought so much joy into your life, they are moments in time which you never want to forget, so remembering them is part of the grieving process.

So, how can memories be so painful when they are so special? I asked a selection of people the answer to that very question, some of the responses were very diverse but equally illustrate the depth of emotion.

"Memories remind me of who I was before Julie died, she was my world and when she left, I didn't know how to carry on without her. My memories remind me of our love and how she made me feel, they make me smile when I think about how we laughed and they make me feel as if I was the luckiest person in the world to have her in my life. My memories make me sad sometimes as I just miss her so, so much, they remind me of what I have lost and what I don't have anymore. I try to make the happy memories the ones which I hold onto as if I focused on the sad ones, I don't think I could live my life as I do."

"When my dad died, the future was just dark, I had no idea how to survive and how I could even start to see a future without him in my life. It's been two years now and my memories now are less intrusive, they don't make me sad all the time, they make me glad of the life he gave me. When I think about my childhood, the day he walked me down the aisle or the day he met his grandson for the first time, it makes me smile. I believe he is with me still, maybe not in person, but he walks with me every day. I sometimes think I can feel him near me and it gives me hope. My memories are what gave me the strength to keep going so for me they are not painful; they are a comfort."

"Grief is the measure of our love, and love hurts. Our brain processes emotional upset with the same brain circuitry that processes physical injury."

"The memories of my beautiful boy were terrible initially, my arms physically ached when I thought about holding him to me. But as time went on it was the memories that comforted me and gave affirmation that he had existed and that he will always be with me (even now 40 years later). I think initially it is the knowledge that you will never have those moments again that tear you apart."

"When we lose someone, we love all we are left with are our memories of them. This becomes painful because when remembering the good times, we long for them again, but with the realisation that we will never be able to have those times again or create new memories, which is hard."

"I have different types of memories about Pete, some of them make me laugh, some make me smile, some make me proud but then there are those that make me sad and some which may make me cry. My happy memories are the ones I instinctively turn to when I think of him, however if I was to sit and really think about the sad memories it would be too upsetting. To this date, I think I still avoid those memories as they still feel quite raw and painful, like the moment I watched him peacefully take his last breath or the moment he told me he loved me before he slipped into unconsciousness."

Memories, as this illustrates are powerful and result in a myriad of different emotions, from sadness to feelings of warmth and adoration.

Many people will never be able to share all of their personal memories, as those are the memories that we keep undisclosed and the ones which we will keep to ourselves forever. It can be important to talk about our experiences and to get the support we need to be able to process grief, yet does that mean we really have to share absolutely everything? I know personally that there are things that I know I will never publicly share.

When thinking about your own memories, especially when you experience a 'trigger', take the time to think about them, acknowledge the emotion whether that be sad or happy, as they are equally important. The triggers will always be there and as much as we can try to evade them, it's incredibly difficult to avoid them completely.

Throughout life's journey, we all develop our own coping strategies and our own unique way of coping with those emotional triggers, however if you feel that you need support with developing those strategies, please consider seeking the support of a professional grief specialist who will support you in your journey.

21

Loss of a Parent

This is Lisa's story, it is one which is incredibly heart-warming but at the same time, heart-breaking. Lisa's journey at the time of writing this story did not involve a bereavement, it was her story following her Mum's diagnosis of Motor Neurone Disease five years previous.

Lisa grew up in a loving family, she was particularly close to her mum, sharing a very special bond with her. Following the diagnosis, Lisa talks about her experience of losing the mum she once knew. It was incredibly upsetting as she watched the symptoms of the disease slowly deteriorate her mums' physical abilities whilst knowing that the mum she loved was very much still there inside.

Sadly, Lisa's mum died in the winter of 2022, she was loved by so many people and will be missed every day by her family and friends.

Although Lisa wrote her story prior to her bereavement she bravely agreed to still share her story as she expressed her wish to raise awareness of Motor Neurone Disease, and in particular the associated loss which the diagnosis and prognosis can bring to family and friends.

This is Lisa's story using her own words, describing her journey.

"I first noticed the change during a family gathering, whilst everyone else seemed to be enjoying the occasion I noticed mum was slurring her speech almost like she was drunk, however mum has never ever been drunk. I thought I was imagining things however when we got home, I spoke to my husband about it, and he said he had noticed it too.

Being a very close extended family, I started to telephone everyone who attended the gathering to ask if they had noticed too. As I spoke to each member of the family in turn, they all said that they had noticed it too but had not mentioned it, this was the first and last time I have ever been angry with my family.

When mum was ultimately diagnosed with MND by the hospital, the realisation of the diagnosis was overwhelming, and I unfortunately suffered a minor break-down in my mental health. I had no idea how to process the life-changing information about my mum, a woman who I love so dearly and am so close to.

When I was younger my next-door neighbours were my 'auntie and uncle'; my uncle Tom was a very strong gentleman who had served in the tank regiment during WW2, he had also served as a Beefeater at the Tower of London. Unfortunately, I remember quite well when he was diagnosed with Motor Neurone Disease as it affected both his mental and physical health. From a strong capable man, he deteriorated rapidly, unable to do anything, unable to speak and unable to care for himself or his wife. He sadly passed away after a couple of years, as quite literally the muscles in his lungs gave up and asphyxiated him. I dread this for my mum; however, I know this may be the terrible future truth.

As time has passed, I have seen first-hand the devastating consequences of this dreadful disease. Although my mum is currently still with us physically and her bra n is as sharp as it ever has been, she is now trapped in a body which can no longer function. Watching mum deteriorate has been devastating especially as I can't be there for all the times I have wanted to. I feel so helpless.

Since I heard about mums' diagnosis I have been struggling, physically, emotionally, and mentally. I wake up regularly at 4am as I know that is the time that most people pass away. I have previously experienced that with my ex-Father-in-law. I sat with him all night and he indeed did pass away at 4am. Personally, I have been self-medicating with alcohol which I know doesn't help however sometimes it helps me forget even just for a while.

I have had many difficult moments, especially now as mum cannot even send me messages as we used to do, her hands get too tired too quickly. When we received the diagnosis, I worked with the MND association to create a word bank for her so she didn't have to sound like the wonderful Stephen Hawkins, however now she can't type in the words so is unable to use it as she would like.

I just hate that I can't help more as I live too far away and have no transport unless my husband is home. I have also had some setbacks as due to the pandemic and my medical issues I have had to isolate which has made it even harder. It has definitely had an effect on my mental health.

I work in care, specifically with young adults who have autism and learning disabilities which is incredibly rewarding but can also be challenging. When out in the community their behaviour can often mean that members of the public look at my clients in a negative way rather than accepting who they are. This can be difficult as they don't understand that they have a condition and that they are still very much wanting to enjoy life.

This makes me think about my mum even more, as one of the things I struggle with most are the reactions of strangers who are often ignorant and (hopefully) unintentionally cruel. I have experienced this all my life however it doesn't get easier. My fellow work colleagues know about mum and how it is affecting my mental health which does offer me a level of support when I need it, however I want to give the care our service users deserve but it exhausts me physically and mentally so I don't feel that I am giving as good care as I would like.

Presently my mum is in a wheelchair, and she can no longer hold her head up or hold in her saliva. When she was able to get out, I often noticed stares and heard muttered comments. Ironically, I think that children are the best. They may ask openly 'what is wrong with that lady' or similar. That I don't mind at all, and I know mum wouldn't either. Those questions are honest and innocent however when their parents may tell them not to stare or try to silence them, I find that really hard. If children are taught at an early age that people have differences, illnesses, or other conditions they will be more likely to accept 'different' people when they grow up.

Personally, I do struggle with negative feelings with my own health suffering as a consequence. Ironically, I don't think that work understands properly how it all affects me and if I am utterly exhausted, they just see me still coming in-to work.

Care is hard at the best of times especially physical care so the choice to use live-in carers for my mum and dad was a difficult transition process, however the carers that have been with my parents have been kind, compassionate and loving, giving my dad some respite from the 24/7 attention he had previously been doing on his own.

The only positive thing I can hang on is that my mum and dad not only have a strong and loving relationship, they also have a great local friend support, we also have a very close and loving extended family. However only mum has a church network. From being children both myself and my sisters have been included in that, however my dad turned away many years ago. That being said the Vicar has been coming over to give mum communion on regular occasions which I know gives her peace although she can't say it.

Since the diagnosis and over the recent months and years I have spoken to a few friends and family, but I have not received any formal support. In the main, I have had support from people in the know such as my friends and family, I hope they know the support I need; it may be anything from a phone call or dragging me out of the house to go for lunch. I have a tendency to hide away when I am not feeling like I can face the world with a happy face. My friends however know sometimes when to 'bully' me in to going out which I really appreciate although I may not initially.

When I think back, when you get a bad diagnosis for someone you love, nothing will ever go back to 'normal'. My mum is still with us, but I will always miss the 'mum' that I have loved since the day I was born. My dad will never stop missing the wife he married and loves so dearly. Life will NEVER be 'normal' again and sadly that is the hardest thing to accept.

Looking forward, honestly, I dread looking to the future. I know that mum will die sometime, probably fairly soon and I don't know how I will cope then. I don't know how I am coping now. When we first got the diagnosis, I was devastated. I still am. How I will cope without her I don't know. How dad will cope I don't know. Somehow, I do know we will all pull together although at this moment I don't know how.

At this present day I am not in a good place and dread that each day may be the last. I have felt that every day since we got the diagnosis. Maybe one day after it happens, I will be able to look back, however at this moment and even as I write this I am in tears, and I am not a teary person normally. However, life doesn't teach you these skills and I am also aware that the experience of grief is different for every person.

Being an older sister to twin sisters we do have some significant special dates throughout the year, including my mum and dad's birthdays being on the same day. I am constantly thinking will mum make it until her birthday? Thankfully she did this year, she also made it to Mother's Day, however, how about Father's Day? How about my twin sisters' birthday or my sister's wedding anniversary? What about her and my dad's 50th Wedding Anniversary which is this year? How about my birthday? I think every special occasion is hard if you lose someone you love and honestly, I don't know how it can be dealt with in advance.

If I were to sit and talk to someone going through a similar experience as myself, I think I would say please say less and listen more, trite words are irrelevant. All I would say is that if we want to talk, you could always be there, although if we don't want to talk that is okay as well. I would never press someone to talk if they don't want to, as sometimes just sitting with your friends or family and saying nothing, just giving support as needed can be enough at that point. Sometimes, when life changes so dramatically it takes time to re-charge and re-think. That may be days, weeks, months, years, decades or forever. Whatever, take your time at your own pace. Feel free to have bad days but also feel free to have good days.

I am still very close to my surviving grandparents, but one thing that always sticks with me is that when my Granny died on her birthday which was the day before mine, someone told me that if someone dies on their birthday, they become an angel. I feel her over me and often talk to her when life is getting hard. She is my guardian angel. I have a very strong faith which is very personal to me, and she keeps me strong."

Lisa's story is one which I feel honoured to have listened to and to be able to share, her bravery in sharing how the 'loss' of her mum following the diagnosis is so life-changing and was incredibly courageous.

I know that Lisa wanted people to read her story to highlight the experience of living with Motor Neurone Disease, from the family's perspective and that if it helped just one person to understand and not feel alone then it would have a beneficial impact.

22

Relationships After Grief

There can be many questions about relationships after a bereavement. Having personal experience of this myself and as a grief specialist, it is a common area of discussion.

There are however a few questions which are difficult, mostly because they are questions with multiple and varied responses, all of which could be relevant, yet equally they are ambiguous. These questions are normally in response to the 'rights or wrongs' about moving on and forming new relationships.

After a bereavement there is no set rule or guideline for new relationships, in fact there is no right or wrong time to feel like you want to start 'going out' or even 'dating' again, everyone is different. People will often ask me, how I personally came to the decision about being in another relationship after Jay died. My answer is always the same, 'it wasn't really an actual fixed decision, it just happened'.

Dating after a bereavement is put simply, 'scary', there are so many emotions which are experienced during that time of change, but one which stands out for many people is the feeling of 'guilt'. It can feel quite overwhelming to feel happiness and love again after a bereavement, yet at the same time, it is a pleasant and heart-warming feeling which allows a person to feel as if a happy and positive future is possible. Unfortunately, the two different perspectives often clash, and it can be incredibly difficult to reach an emotional consensus on how you move forward.

After a loved one dies, it can be hard to imagine the future, you have no idea how to live your life without them and it is difficult to contemplate how it is remotely possible to even begin to love someone as much as you loved before grief entered the new world you live in.

One of the most dominant and emotionally confusing thought-processes can be how you accept what other people think of your decision to be in another relationship, with opinions and acceptance being the two common concerns. These can be quite difficult to overcome at times.

There are many people, including family, friends and acquaintances who will offer their sincere and loving support to 'moving on' and finding happiness, however there are also those who may be less receptive.

You often experience both sides of that conundrum. You can be lucky enough to have many if not all your family and friends who support you, however there may also be those who don't agree. There may be many times when it can be incredibly upsetting to hear from those who do not approve of your decisions.

For those people who know you well, there is no question that your love for the person who died is any less, yet their support in your new beginning is an important step forward. If the person who died was young, there is also an element of knowing that although your heart has been broken by the bereavement, it has many more years of love still to give.

Personally, my husband Gareth did indeed win my heart and in 2022 we were happily married. He knows and understands my grief and is 100% supportive of my experiences; he understands because he knows I love him for being him, just like he loves me for being me. I often say to Gareth that I will always love Jay but I can't be 'in love' with him, as he's not here. Although I will always love Jay, my heart is now cared for by Gareth, I feel incredibly blessed to have him in my life and to know that he holds my heart, knowing that it has emotional scars.

My personal story is unique to me, but it also echoes the story of many I speak with every day. Whether it is your own personal feelings about starting a new relationship or the thoughts of others, it can be both detrimental and empowering in its effect, in my case it was a bit of both.

Loving someone again, does not mean forgetting about the past and all the wonderful memories of your loved one, those memories are who you are and anyone who loves you will understand that although the grief does not define who you are, it is very much a part of you.

Even when you start a new relationship, the memories and triggers do not disappear, they will always be there and there will always be those special memory dates in the year when you know will be a little overwhelming and sad. To get through those times, the best advice I can give is simply to go with what you feel works for you. Take the time to reflect if you need it, go for a walk, visit a special place or maybe keeping busy is what feels right for you, truth is there is no right or wrong answer.

Being in a new relationship does not mean you erase or forget about the past, that's impossible to do, instead your life finds a way of living beside the grief and the memories in a way that allows you to move forward.

It is such a personal decision about when the time is right to think about another relationship and there really is no definitive answer, but follow your heart and try to remember what 'you' want rather than what other people may think or want for you. I'm not going to lie; it is incredibly hard, and I personally have cried many, many nights trying to come to terms with my decisions but it was when I started to follow my heart that I found happiness.

Truth is, there are some people who may not agree with your decisions and those comments, opinions and thoughts do sometimes hurt, but they can also be empowering and if you truly find love then those feelings of guilt are offset by the happiness of the future which lies ahead of you.

23

So... What Is 'Normal'?

So, what is normal? Can we go back to normal? Or, is it just that we take a step back and look to create a new normal after a loss or bereavement?

Life after loss and/or a bereavement can be demanding, both physically and emotionally and although I would very much like to offer advice on how you start that 'new-normal' journey, its advice which is not truly mine to give. The reason for that, is that every journey is unique, so there isn't a 'one size fits all' answer, we find our own future, our own way of moving forward, in our own way.

My own journey has been one of many personal achievements in both my personal and professional career, however it has also been one of uncertainty and learning from my failures. The reason for that is simple, it is because that is what is 'normal'.

'Normal' is getting things wrong, 'normal' is feeling overwhelmed at times, but 'normal' is also learning to live again and finding yourself again in a new world and realising that it's okay to be happy and to even love again. More importantly it is about creating your own meaningful future.

Loss, bereavement, death and dying are words which can be life changing so going 'back to normal' after experiencing one or more of them, is highly ambiguous. My advice to anyone who has read this book, seeking answers to how to 'get over' grief or loss is that I hope you have found your own sense to what 'normal' really means to you.

I hope that you can find an inner strength to look towards a meaningful future whilst at the same time reflecting and having a sense of finding comfort in your memories. Never be afraid to ask for support. Support is not a sign of weakness; it is a sign of an inner strength you never knew you had until you needed to call on it.

Grief is a journey and it is a journey which no one really wants to ever experience but for those of us that do find ourselves on that journey, there is hope and you can with support and time find a way through to your own 'new normal'.

Final Words

This book has been a journey through so many different emotions. At the heart of the book are the contributors who kindly and bravely shared their story. I use 'bravery' with such a heavy heart as I know that most of the stories were shared due to personal loss and/or bereavement, but I also feel privileged to have had the opportunity to have been gifted the opportunity to hear and share each and every journey.

When I began this book, I had no idea really where it would take me and if people would trust me with their inner most feelings and thoughts in talking about such personal experiences, but they did and I find it hard to express how grateful I am for their raw honesty, it has been astounding.

Intertwined within the book is my own personal story. This has been my driving force not just throughout the writing of the book but over the last few years. I am sadly not unique in my experience, there are thousands if not millions of people who experience loss, bereavement, and grief on a daily basis across the world. Although it is shared global emotion, every single person's story is unique to them which is why 'normal' is not quite the simple words you once thought!

If you ever find yourself doubting that you won't get through those difficult days, I would love you to pick up this book again and re-read it. Life can be difficult, and it can be hard to imagine getting through to tomorrow, never mind a future, but it is possible.

The feelings of grief or loss never leave you, instead they remind us of how much love we give to one another, and how taking time to find yourself and coming together when we need to, really makes a difference to that journey.

"Pay attention to how you feel each day. Taking that first step can be difficult but the strength you find to keep going is often surprising. Strive daily to challenge negative thoughts which rob you of your confidence and resilience.

Positivity and change will help you bring more happiness into your life, but it takes time, support and a bucket full of stoicism. Remember that you cannot change other people and how they act or think, but we can change ourselves. Be kind to yourself and never give up hope. The hope is still inside you; it just needs the time to heal and it will find a way to shine bright once again".

The Heart Plaster

Grief is like an emotional wound to the heart.

Imagine you have a wound to your heart; it is bleeding and it hurts so you put a plaster on it. The bleeding stops and for a while the plaster is covering the wound. On the outside, there are no longer any visible signs of the wound (pain of your grief) but underneath, the pain is very real and the heart feels broken.

Now, imagine taking that plaster straight off... the result would be that your heart has not healed and it will then continue to bleed and be painful. Like a wound, grief takes time to heal, we need time to get over the pain and the initial shock of our loss and we cannot just simply 'get over it'.

Like a wound, if we simply left our wounded heart unattended, the pain may increase or get worse, so sometimes, we need a little extra help to help us recover and just like a physical wound, we sometimes need a little more support to help us through the healing process. Talking to a bereavement counsellor, a support service, a friend or family member can be part of that healing process.

Over time, you can start to take off the plaster, a little bit at a time. When the plaster comes off completely, the initial pain may have lowered but there is a scar left by the grief and that scar stays with us for life. Occasionally, when something triggers our grief, the scar hurts for a while and we are reminded of our loss and the pain we felt and still feel.

Our emotional scars make us who we are, they are a reminder of the grief we have experienced but also, they are a reminder of the physical and emotional strength it takes to heal after a bereavement.

References

Collins English Dictionary, 2022. (online) Available at: https://www.collinsdictionary.com/dictionary/english/loss, (accessed 19/2/22)

Available worldwide from Amazon

Michael Terence
Publishing

www.mtp.agency

mtp.agency

@mtp_agency

Printed in Great Britain
by Amazon

27814051R00093